D0425872

STRANGE ATTRACTORS

Other books by William Sleator

STRANGE ATTRACTORS

WILLIAM SLEATOR

E. P. DUTTON   NEW YORK

The author would like to acknowledge Rachel Foster, whose computer made it impossible for him to escape from this book when he was away from home.

Library of Congress Cataloging-in-Publication Data

Sleator, William.
    Strange attractors / William Sleator.—1st ed.
        p.   cm.
    Summary: Max finds himself in possession of a time-travel device which is eagerly sought by two desperate men, the scientist who invented it and the scientist's alter ego from a different timeline.
        ISBN 0-525-44530-7
        [1. Time travel—Fiction.   2. Science fiction.]   I. Title.
PZ7.S6313St   1990   89-33840
[Fic]—dc20   CIP
                                                              AC

Published in the United States by E. P. Dutton, a division of Penguin Books USA Inc.

Published simultaneously in Canada by Fitzhenry & Whiteside Limited, Toronto

Editor: Ann Durell   Designer: Barbara Powderly
Printed in U.S.A.   First Edition
10 9 8 7 6 5 4 3 2 1

This book is for my mother,
whose encouragement and example
gave me the confidence to be an oddball,
for which I will always be grateful.

"You don't look like you're feeling much better, Max," Mom said when I came down to breakfast.

"Better than what?" I didn't know what she was talking about.

"And why are you dressed like that? I didn't expect to see you in that getup again for the rest of the summer."

"What do you mean, *again?*" It was the first time I had worn the new blue sport coat we'd bought the day before. I sat down and reached for the cornflakes. "You're the one who said I had to wear this today. I'm going to Mercury Labs, remember?"

Dad looked up from the paper. "You didn't tell us they invited you back," he said.

What was the matter with them? "How can they invite me back if I've never been there?" I dumped cornflakes into my bowl, wondering if they thought they were being funny.

I'd been looking forward to this visit to Mercury Labs— a special honor for top science students—for months. It was a week after my graduation from high school, and I was prepared. I knew about some of the work that was being done there, especially by a guy named Sylvan in the field of nonlinear temporal dynamics. I had only been able to get a look at one of his papers—the rest of his work was highly classified—but it had excited me a lot. The scientific reality of time travel was something I had always wanted to believe in, and the more I had looked at Sylvan's paper, the more it seemed his complicated equations demonstrated that time travel was actually possible, though he never said it in so many words.

"You went to Mercury Labs yesterday, Max," Mom said, staring at me over her coffee cup.

"Cut it out." I sprinkled sugar on the cornflakes.

"Still feeling disoriented, huh?" she asked me.

"What do you mean, disoriented? I feel great." But I didn't feel great; I had a headache, and their peculiar behavior was confusing me. "I have to hurry," I said. "The security there is fierce, and if I get there later than the rest of the group, they won't let me in."

"He really *doesn't* remember," Mom said, looking at Dad. She turned to me, frowning, and I realized that she wasn't joking, she was dead serious. "You went to Mercury Labs yesterday, Max. You got sick in the middle of the tour and had to come home. You went straight to bed. I guess you're not completely over it yet."

"What are you talking about? Today's June 24, the day of the tour." But she sounded so sure of herself that I felt a twinge of fear. I checked my watch. The date was June 25. My heart began to pound.

They glanced at each other. Then Dad showed me the paper. It also said June 25.

"But this is crazy!" I began to panic. "How can it be June 25? Yesterday was June 23. We bought the jacket. I didn't get sick. The lab visit is *today!*" But my head was throbbing worse than ever.

"I guess you'll have to see the doctor after all," Mom said. "You've been sleeping since they brought you home yesterday afternoon. I hoped you'd get over it, but I'll make an appointment right away."

I stood up abruptly. "I never went to Mercury Labs!" I insisted. "I'm not going to any doctor; I'm going to the labs."

The phone rang.

Mom hurried to answer it, her eyes on me. "Oh, hello. Yes, he's here." She held out the phone. "For you, Max. It's the girl you met at the labs, the one who phoned last night."

What girl? Girls never called me up. As I lifted the phone, I noticed that the jacket seemed a little heavy on one side—was my calculator in the pocket?—but I was too preoccupied to pay any attention to it now. "Hello?"

"Hi, handsome," said a totally unfamiliar female voice.

"I hope you're feeling better today," she went on, without giving me a chance to speak. She sounded concerned; her voice was deep, firm, confident. "I've been worrying about you. We were having such a wonderful time, everything you said was so fascinating. And then suddenly you just . . ." Her words faded in the middle of the sentence.

I couldn't pretend I knew who she was; I've never been any good at lying. "Listen, I . . . Who are you?" I asked her. The reality of what had happened was finally beginning to sink in. All the evidence indicated that I really had been to Mercury Labs yesterday and forgotten it, frightening and unbelievable as it seemed. "Did I really meet you at the labs? I don't remember anything about yesterday at all."

"You don't *remember?*" she said very slowly. "You don't remember anything about the labs, or about . . . ?"

It was funny the way she kept leaving her sentences unfinished; it didn't tally with that confident voice. I wondered if she expected me to finish the sentences for her. "I don't remember anything after going to bed the night before last," I told her.

"Wait. Hold on a second," she said, sounding excited. I could hear her talking to somebody, but the voices were muffled, as though she had her hand over the phone. Then she said, "In that case you *have* to come over, Max, right away. We can talk about it. Maybe if I tell you what happened your memory will come back." She paused. "And, uh, be sure to bring anything you might have picked up at the labs," she said carefully. "That's really important, in terms of bringing back your memory. Okay?"

I hadn't noticed anything I could have picked up at the labs, but I was extremely curious to find out what had happened there. "Come over? Sure, I guess I can come over," I said. "Except . . . who are you? Where do you live?"

"Oh!" She laughed, a little longer than seemed necessary. "That's right, you've forgotten. I'm Eve, Eve Sylvan. My father is a scientist at the labs."

Sylvan! That was the name of the guy who wrote the paper on nonlinear temporal dynamics. Did I really meet him, talk to him? Suddenly I was more excited than scared. "Sylvan, from Mercury Labs? He's your *father?*"

"Yes, he's my father," she said, as though it were a stupid question. "I was there yesterday, when your group came in. You have a pencil?" She reeled off an address in a neighboring suburb. "And don't forget to bring . . . what you found yesterday."

Mom and Dad were doubtful when I asked for the car. "I'm not sure you're well enough to drive," Mom said. "And I want you to go to the doctor."

"But they want me to come over right away, so they can help me remember what happened. Her father's a scientist at the labs; he does really interesting stuff. I guess I was talking to them yesterday."

They were still reluctant, but the fact that her father was an important scientist—and had been there when I got sick—finally won them over.

"Just let me have the jacket," Mom said as she handed me the car keys. "I want to take it to the cleaners and get that stain out right away."

"Sure," I said, shrugging it off, noticing for the first time the stain on the right sleeve. I ran upstairs to check my room, just to see if I really had brought anything back from the labs. There was nothing unfamiliar there, and only the usual items in my protopack, the leather pouch I wear around my waist to hold my wallet, calculator, keys, and other necessities. As I was on my way out the door the phone rang, but I didn't wait. I was eager to get to the Sylvans' house, and the phone call probably wasn't for me anyway.

Eve's directions brought me to a neighborhood of mansions. The house was not visible from the road, the asphalt driveway curving away into a little wood. The name TAYLOR was printed on the mailbox, not Sylvan. I pulled over and checked the directions again, along with the number on the mailbox; this seemed to be the right address, so I turned in.

The starkly modern, poured-concrete house spread itself out over a sloping lawn. Balconies sprouted from different levels. I stopped the car in a round paved area at the end of the drive, beside a sleek new silver Jeep Cherokee—the most expensive model. I wondered briefly why it was parked precisely within an area outlined in white paint. As I walked up the flagstone path, I heard the sound of water and saw that a large balcony on the right side of the house was cantilevered out over a waterfall. The building obviously had been designed by an architect to fit spectacularly into this site. I wondered again if I was at the wrong address. My father was a scientist at the university, but none of his colleagues lived in a house like this. I'd never seen anything like it. If this *was* the right place, Eve's father had to be a real big shot. Maybe he earned royalties from some kind of invention. I rang the bell.

The door opened instantly. A girl stood in the hallway, on a floor of polished black stone. She was as tall as I was, her head held high like a dancer's. She gazed at me. "Max! Welcome," she said, and looked me quickly up and down. Her eyes stopped for a moment on my proto-pack, then moved back to my face.

They were gray eyes, carefully outlined with dark makeup, which made them seem very large. She had prominent cheekbones and a small nose; her skin glowed with health. But it was her mouth that gave the arresting quality to her face. Her lower lip was full, her upper lip thin and sculptured, the shape emphasized by red lipstick. Short, streaked blond hair crinkled around her head in an unruly halo. I'd never seen anyone like her.

"What's the matter?" she said.

I realized I'd been standing there staring at her. "Matter? Nothing's . . . I mean, well, it just seems strange," I said awkwardly. "I must have met you yesterday, but I *feel* like I've never seen you before. It's weird."

"You really don't remember me at all?" she said, as though she found it hard to believe that anyone could forget her.

I shook my head.

"I can't *stand* it that you don't remember me!" She stared at me, her lips parted, her expression somehow conveying a feeling of barely controlled wildness. "We'll *have* to fix that! Come on, sit down." She pushed the door shut, then swung around and walked past me, moving as smoothly as a cat in her shiny black jumpsuit. "But first just give me what you . . ." She turned back and looked at me.

"Give you what?" I asked.

She stopped, not smiling now. "You know, the . . . what you took with you from the labs. I *told* you to bring it." Her tone was peremptory.

"I didn't take anything from the labs. I looked around at home but there was nothing."

"It's not in your pack?" she demanded, frowning at me now.

"No, it's not. Why should it be? Why do you think I took something from the labs? Is it missing? Did you see me leave with it? What happened at the labs, anyway?" I was more impatient than ever to find out.

"Go in there and sit down," she said, waving at an opening on the right. "I'll get some, uh, some soda. You must be thirsty. . . . "

I wandered into a large room, which seemed to be the living room, though it was almost empty except for a long black leather couch against one wall. Did that mean they had just moved into this house? Was that why the wrong name was on the mailbox? Drawn by the sound of the waterfall, I pushed open the glass doors across from the couch, stepped out onto the balcony, and looked down over the concrete railing at the noisy cascade below.

I followed the motion of individual bubbles as they were swept along toward the waterfall, trying to see the water not as a solid mass, but as an intricate network of wildly crisscrossing pathways. I'd always looked at rushing water that way; my head moved back and forth, watching the fate of the little bubbles as they hit the falls.

"Do you like lemon or lime in your soda, Max?"

I turned around quickly. Eve stepped out onto the balcony, smiling again. "Lemon or lime, Max?" she repeated, standing so close to me that I could see her individual eyelashes, thickened by mascara.

"Uh, lime, I guess."

"Max," she said softly, her voice barely audible above the waterfall. She reached out and touched my hand gently. Her fingers were cool. "Don't be so antsy, Max," she said. "We'll get your memory back."

I didn't know what to say.

"I'll never forget yesterday," she went on. "And I don't want you to forget it either." She squeezed my hand briefly. "Be back in a sec." She moved quickly into the house.

I stood and looked after her until she was out of the living room, then turned reluctantly and rested my arms on the railing. But I didn't see the waterfall now; I saw Eve. Suddenly, without understanding why, I wanted more than anything to impress her.

Something moved at the edge of my vision and I looked up from the water. A man whirled through the air in a fast double somersault and vanished below the edge of another balcony.

The waterfall pounded below me; the man shot silently into the air again, his knees bent. He must have been jumping on a trampoline, and he was not a novice. Something distracted him. His head jerked up, away from me, his legs started to uncurl. He dropped below the balcony and did not reappear.

What was going on here? Was that her father, Sylvan, the scientist, unlikely as it seemed? I stretched out over the edge, trying to see more, but he wasn't jumping now, and the back of the house was hidden by the far balcony wall. I stepped back inside, pulling the door shut behind me.

And I saw that there was a picture in the living room after all, a single long, narrow panel hanging above the couch, stretching the full length of the wall. A chaotic bifurcation graph. Period doubling was what this graph was all about, and period doubling fascinated me.

I'd seen graphs of this process before in books, but never one so large, or so finely detailed. The action moved from left to right, beginning with a single black line against a white background, emerging from the left edge of the graph. After about a foot, the line forked, or bifurcated. Now there were two lines, curving gently apart as they moved across the center of the space; the graph had entered period two. Soon both lines split again, making four lines. But period four was shorter than period two, and quickly the lines divided again into eight, then more quickly into sixteen, thirty-two—and suddenly into chaos.

I moved closer. The right side of the picture had become an expanding, fuzzy area of gray, the individual lines difficult to follow because there were so many of them. The line had been sucked into the so-called chaotic veil, in which there were cascades of bifurcations, an insanity of infinite forkings, random, unpredictable. By falling under the control of something scientists call a strange attractor, the graph had evolved into a web of disorder and confusion from which theoretically it could never escape, even if computers continued to plot the process to the end of time.

I tried again to follow one of the individual forking paths, but lost it instantly. And suddenly I was struck by a strange sensation of hopelessness: once the first bifurcation had happened, chaos seemed inevitable. And I was in that chaos, pitching down into the tangled grayish haze. It was a sickening feeling, but there was also an odd, exciting edge to it that startled me. I started to turn away from it, then saw something in the chaotic area that I hadn't noticed. I stepped closer again.

"Some soda, Max?"

Eve stood just inside the room, her exotic haloed head

tilted to the side, her large gray eyes fixed on me. She held two frosty glasses of ice and sparkling dark liquid. How long had she been watching me?

She handed me a glass and shrugged at the graph. "That thing is called a bifurcation diagram, or something," she said.

"I know," I said. "But I never knew there was that area of stability in the middle of chaos."

"Period three," said a man's voice.

The red-haired man who had been spinning on the trampoline a moment ago was standing beside her now, a head taller than her, shirtless in a pair of running shorts, his body firm and youthful. But why was he wearing a pack around his waist? His was not leather like mine, but constructed of some kind of yellow plastic, with no zipper I could see on it.

"But period three is only a brief window of stability," he continued, his handsome, square-jawed face engaging in its enthusiasm. He pointed a pack of cigarettes at the graph. "From period three, the strange attractor drags the three lines right back into chaos again, faster than before. It's actually a very interesting strange attractor. Want to see some blowups I have? I could find them in a—"

"Oh, Dad, not *now*," Eve said, sighing. "Max needs to get his memory back, remember?" She gestured at the black leather couch. "Sit down, Max. Relax."

It was more like an order than an invitation, and I complied automatically, feeling clumsy as I sank down into the deep cushions. The couch was very low, the kind that it is almost a struggle to get up from. The two tall,

13

athletic people stared down at me. "Sure you don't want a hit of gin in that drink?" her father asked me, grinning.

"Uh, no, thanks," I said, slightly shocked that he would offer me alcohol this early in the day—not to mention, I was under the legal age.

"So you really don't remember anything about what happened yesterday?" Sylvan asked me.

"Nothing," I told him, as Eve sat down on the couch and lit a cigarette.

"I'm surprised the graph didn't bring anything back to you," he said slowly, watching me. "Looking at it now, didn't it remind you of anything about yesterday? Not even an emotional response?"

I remembered my peculiar reaction to the graph. "Actually, the graph *did* give me a funny feeling, now that you mention it," I said. I turned to Eve, then back to Sylvan. "It scared me. The chaotic veil seemed really *horrible* somehow, sickening—but also exciting. I felt kind of like . . . I was falling into it just now. As if the strange attractor that pulls the system into chaos was pulling at me, too."

Their eyes met. And the phone rang, a piercing jolt in the bare concrete house.

Eve sprang to her feet, cigarette in hand, moving toward the phone. "It must be that crank caller. I'll take care of—"

The phone rang again.

"No. Let me handle it," Sylvan said, his voice suddenly urgent.

The phone rang a third time. There was a click.

14

"Hello," began the clearly audible recorded message: "No one is home now, but—"

"Be right back, Max!" Eve said, and they both rushed from the room.

What was the matter with them? I was more confused than ever. If they were so sure it was a crank caller, you'd think they'd just ignore it, and let the machine take care of it.

Unless, that is, they didn't want me to hear the message the caller was going to leave.

And then I saw the folded piece of paper on the couch where Eve had been sitting. It must have fallen out of her pocket.

3

I didn't have much time. They could be back in an instant. I quickly unfolded the paper. It was a piece of stationery from Mercury Labs. Underneath the green Mercury Labs logo were the words HONOR SCIENCE STUDENTS, June 24, in high-quality laser printing, followed by a list of names, with addresses and phone numbers. There were penciled check marks beside most of the names. But beside my name was a star, and the scribbled words, *Left early*. And next to that, in red capitals, apparently written at another time with another pencil, was the single word, *AMNESIA!*

I heard footsteps. I folded the paper, slipped it between the cushions, and got to my feet, clumsily, because the couch was so low. I turned, and tried to look as though I'd been studying the graph.

Eve strolled into the room. "You've been having problems with crank callers?" I asked.

She shrugged. "It's no big deal."

"Then why did you both run out of the room?" I continued, in my usual blunt way.

"None of your business," she snapped, glaring at me.

Sylvan strode into the room with a bottle of beer. "I see you wear a pack too, Max," he said, without preamble. "Convenient for picking things up, isn't it? What have you got in it now?"

"Why do you want to know what's in my pack?" I asked. If he could be brusque, so could I. "I mean, it's none of your business what I've got in here."

"I thought you said you didn't bring it!" Eve cried out.

"And maybe it *is* my business," her father said roughly. He put down the bottle and moved toward me, reaching out his hand. His face was flushed, his crew-cut hair damp at the edges. "Open it up, please."

I backed away from him, frightened by his sudden change in manner. Before he left the room he had been charming and relaxed; now he was aggressive, on the attack, and he wasn't hiding it. My hand moved automatically to cover the protopack. "What's the matter with you?" I said. "Why do you want to know what's in my pack? If you'd just tell me what happened yesterday, maybe . . . maybe I could help you find whatever it is you're looking for."

"You know it's mine, Max!" Sylvan was almost shouting now. "Hand it over."

"But why should I?" I demanded, my voice rising too. "And why won't you tell me what happened yesterday?"

"Give me what's in your pack and I'll tell you," Sylvan said, staring hard at me, still approaching.

I backed up against the wall.

He was close enough to grab me, both arms lifted in a fighter's stance, the veins standing out on his large muscular hands.

"All right, all right!" I undid the strap on the protopack, pulled it off my belt, and unzipped it. I took out my calculator, wallet, Swiss Army knife, pens and pencils, pocket flashlight, throwing them onto the couch one by one. I thrust the empty protopack into his hand.

He reached inside it, scrabbled around, then looked back at me. "But . . ." He blinked, his eyes the same gray shade as Eve's. "But it's empty. It's not in here."

"I told you, I do *not* have anything from the labs." I said it with absolute conviction. It was not until the words were out of my mouth that I remembered the unusual weight in my jacket pocket when I had answered the phone earlier this morning.

Sylvan turned to Eve. "Maybe . . . maybe we made a mistake," he said, and cleared his throat.

But they hadn't made a mistake. Now it seemed that I really *could* have taken something from the labs—something they desperately wanted, something that was now at the cleaners. I opened my mouth to tell them.

But I stopped—because of what Sylvan had just said

about making a mistake. How could they think they had made a mistake if they had been there yesterday when I took this thing? Was it possible that they weren't really sure I was the one who had it? I thought of the list that had fallen out of Eve's pocket.

"But, Max," Eve said, pleading with me, "it *has* to be you, because . . . " Her voice faded.

"Because what? What's going on here anyway?" Suddenly I was angry; all at once it was clear that they were hiding something from me, trying to get this thing away from me without telling me what had happened yesterday. "Why won't you just tell me the truth instead of . . . of playing these stupid games, threatening me like this?"

Sylvan quickly stepped away from me, his hands falling to his sides. He picked up the beer and took a long swallow, back to his normal self now, as though a minute ago he hadn't been about to attack me. "I think your condition is a little more serious than we realized," he said, his tone bland and conversational. "It might be dangerous— for you—if we just tell you what you've forgotten. You should see a neurologist. Fugal amnesia, I think they call it—the brain running from something too terrible to remember. I now see that it could be disastrous if we remind you what it is, without knowing what we're doing. What you need is some fun." His face lit up. "So how about trying the trampoline? You'll love the sensation."

"We could go for a swim," Eve urged me, smiling, shaking back her hair. "We have a great water slide. You don't need a suit."

19

"I see. You're not going to tell me." I was more furious than ever. "Can I have my protopack, please?" Sylvan handed it to me. I strapped it on, put the stuff back inside it, and walked out of the living room.

Eve followed me. "What are you going to do now?" she asked.

I headed for the door, not looking at her. "I don't know. Go home. Go to a *neurologist*. What do you care?"

"Wait a minute, Max!" She pulled at my arm.

I turned to face her. "Yeah?"

There was something different about the way she was looking at me now. Her voice dropped to a whisper, as if she didn't want her father to hear. "You know, I think I like you . . . I mean *really* like you," she said, with a little laugh, as though she was surprised at herself. "The way you got so mad just now, even when Dad bullied you. The way you don't hide your feelings." She paused, still holding onto my arm. "Will you call me as soon as you get home? And don't do anything stupid. I'm worried about you." And she leaned forward and kissed me on the lips.

It was so unexpected that I forgot how angry I was. Without thinking, I kissed her back, squeezing her hand.

And then it was over and I was out the door, driving away, still feeling the sensation of her lips, still smelling her perfume.

I didn't understand what was going on, what they were looking for, why they wouldn't tell me what had happened yesterday. But one thing I did know for sure: I had to see this girl again. Why was I driving away from her?

All I wanted was to turn around, go back, and be with her.

I thought again of the weight in my jacket pocket this morning. Was it really the object they were looking for? If so, and if I could get my hands on it, should I give it to them? Or should I first try to find out what it was? If it *was* what they were looking for, that would give me an excuse to call Eve, to see her again.

Mom's car was not in the driveway. I rushed into the house to see if she had taken anything out of the jacket pocket before going to the cleaners. There was still nothing unusual in my room, or in any of the other places she would have left it.

But there was a message on the pad beside the kitchen phone. "Call Eve—*very important!*" Mom had written in her messy scrawl, with a number below it. I smiled. Eve *was* worried about me. I dialed quickly, not bothering to decipher the other scribbles on the pad.

She answered at the beginning of the first ring, as though she'd been waiting by the phone.

"Hi, it's Max."

"Max! I'm so glad you finally called," she said in her firm, confident voice. "We've been—"

"Eve, listen, I'm sorry I didn't tell you, but I was so confused. I *do* have that thing from the labs, I think."

"*What?*" She sounded horrified. "You mean your jacket isn't at the cleaners?"

I stared blankly at the phone. I knew I had never said anything to her about the jacket.

"Max, say something! Isn't it at the cleaners?"

Too confused to answer, I glanced down at the note again. And I saw that Mom had written at the bottom, "She called twice, at 9 and 10."

But I had been with her, at her house, at 10 o'clock.

4

"Who is this?" I said. "You're not Eve Sylvan. I *know* her. I was at her house this morning."

There was a long silence. Then she said, in a dead voice, "Oh, God, they already found you . . ."

In the next instant she was practically screaming. "You didn't give them anything, did you? You didn't tell them what—"

"*Who* found me?" I interrupted her. "What are you talking about? Who are you, anyway?"

"*I'm* Eve Sylvan and I've got to have the receipt for the

jacket your mother took to the cleaners this morning."

My mind began to function again. "How can you be Eve Sylvan? And what makes you think my mother took my jacket to the cleaners?"

"Because you stained it, on the sleeve, when you were with me and my father at the labs yesterday. Now do you believe me?"

"I don't know. But let's say I do agree to get the receipt. Then shouldn't I just try to pick up the jacket, and the . . . the thing in the pocket?"

"No!" The thought of that seemed to terrify her. "Don't go anywhere near the cleaners. It's not safe; the others are dangerous, and they might be following you. Just bring me the receipt."

"But what's this all about? Who *are* they? And how do I know this thing you want doesn't really belong to them and *not* you?"

"Did *they* tell you what happened yesterday?"

"No," I admitted, suddenly realizing they had told me absolutely nothing. And this girl *did* know about the jacket.

"Well, we *will* tell you. Trust me, Max. Don't go near the cleaners. Don't tell anybody anything, including your parents. Just get the receipt and bring it. You have a pencil? Here's our address."

As soon as I hung up I checked the phone book. The only Sylvan listed had the number I had just called, and the same address in the city that the girl on the phone had just given me.

Mom came home soon after that, and I had no trouble

explaining to her that I had left my calculator in the jacket pocket and had come back from Eve's to try to get it from the cleaners. All I needed was the receipt. Then I could try to get the calculator and go back to Eve's and finish finding out what had happened at the labs. I felt a little funny telling this story to Mom, but it wasn't a real lie.

Because I did go directly to the cleaners with the receipt, ignoring the warning of the girl on the phone.

Yes, she had the right listing in the phone book and had promised to tell me everything. But I had no evidence that she would. On the phone, she hadn't told me much more than the others; just ordered me around the way they had. I felt like a pawn, and I didn't like it. Once I gave up the receipt, I might never find out what was really going on, what they were looking for.

And was it possible that what they were looking for had something to do with Sylvan's classified research on non-linear temporal dynamics? This might be my only chance to find out.

So I took the receipt to the cleaners, making sure no Jeep Cherokee was following me. And yes, the woman did remember the jacket with the object sewn into the inner pocket. It had taken her quite a while to get it out before sending off the jacket to the central cleaning plant, she grumbled. But she had been smart enough to attach a copy of the receipt to the object, which she had kept in a safe place at the back of the store. She handed it over without argument when I showed her my receipt. I took the object, thanked her quickly, checked outside for the Jeep Cherokee again, then locked myself in the car.

The object looked sort of like a clunky, old-fashioned calculator, about five inches long and an inch thick, with a display screen and a small array of keys. What was unusual about it was that it seemed homemade, not mass-produced. The surface was rough and unpolished. I could see the little screws holding the metal plates together, and in a couple of places the edges were not joined perfectly, leaving narrow gaps through which the mess of wires and chips on the inside was partly visible. There was a piece of electrical tape covering a bump at the bottom of the key panel. I thought for a moment, then carefully pulled off the tape.

I was right. The tape had been covering an On/Off switch to prevent the power from being accidentally turned on. I studied the panel more carefully. There were numbered keys from 0 through 9, a decimal point, and a couple of keys with labels I didn't understand: ARRIVAL TIME and DEPARTURE TIME. Above the display was a strip of some rough material that looked a little like Velcro.

I pushed the On/Off switch just to see what would happen, figuring I couldn't get into any trouble if I didn't push any of the other keys.

The date and time came on across the top of the display: first the year, followed by the month, the day, the hours, minutes, and the seconds ticking away. It was a 24-hour clock, on which 13:17 meant 1:17 P.M. Below the clock appeared the words *Enter specimen code or new sample* in fuzzy, low-resolution amber letters.

I stared at the display, trying to figure out what it meant. The screen was a little smudged, and I licked my finger and started to polish it. My finger brushed across the Velcro-like surface. I felt a slight electric shock, and almost cried out. *New Specimen: 15.1. Enter* DEPARTURE TIME appeared on the display.

Did that mean *I* was registered on the thing now as Specimen 15.1? I didn't like the thought of that. I immediately switched it off, zipped it into the protopack, and drove quickly out of the parking lot.

I tried to be as logical as possible about what was happening, and what I should do with the object in my protopack. The people I met that morning had told me nothing about the previous day—they had given me no evidence that they had met me at the labs, or that they had ever seen me before. They must have found my name and number from the list in Eve's pocket. The wrong name was on their mailbox; the house looked as though they had just moved into it. And her father, when he saw that I had nothing unusual in my protopack, said that maybe they had made a mistake.

They had to be impostors, it all added up. They were trying to get their hands on the object in my protopack, an invention of the real Sylvan, whose house I was driving to now. The real Sylvan must have hidden it on me, because of something that had happened at the labs yesterday. And once the object was back safely where it belonged, these dangerous impostors would have no more interest in me; I would be safe from them. So why did that make me feel oddly disappointed?

The new Eve—the real Eve—had told me to leave it at the cleaners. The right thing to do, once I was sure it really did belong to them, would be to confess right away that I had picked it up, and give it back to them. But I was reluctant to do that, because then I'd probably never find out what it really was, or anything else about Sylvan's intriguing and classified research. So what *was* I going to do with the object when I got to their house?

The address she had given me turned out to be a large, ornate apartment building—with round turrets, a crenellated roof, and a facade covered with carvings, curlicues upon curlicues. It was dark inside the lobby, and a little shabby, and there was that old apartment-house smell. As I pressed the buzzer with the name SYLVAN beside it, I thought with regret of the trampoline and the pool. Now I wished I had gone for a swim this morning; I wished I had stayed longer with that other girl, whom I would probably never see again. I sighed. The real Eve and Sylvan couldn't possibly be anywhere near as interesting and attractive as the impostors.

"Who is it?" said the voice on the intercom.

"Max."

"Look into the camera."

Old as this building was, it was equipped with an up-to-date video screening device. I stared self-consciously into the lens.

"I'll be right down."

A moment later the inner door opened.

The girl was just a little shorter than I because of the relaxed way she carried her body. She wore a loose, sleeveless blue dress. Her pale face was devoid of makeup; her long, dark-blondish hair was pulled back into a thick braid that hung down to the middle of her back.

But she was the same girl I had met this morning.

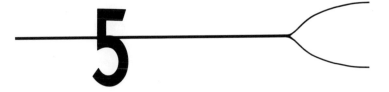

5

"Come on in, Max. Did you bring the receipt?"

I stared at her without moving. The same gray eyes, small nose, thinly sculptured upper lip. The same girl.

"What's the matter?" she asked.

"You put on a wig," I murmured. "You changed clothes and washed off your makeup and drove here before I even got home and . . ." I shook my head. "No. There wasn't time. You couldn't have done all that before I called. And that's not a wig. Are you twins or something? *Now* what are you trying to pull?"

She put her hand to her mouth. "Is . . . is *she* really that much like me?"

"Don't you know? How can you be somebody's twin and not know what they look like? Were you separated at birth or something? But that doesn't make sense either, because then you would have . . ." I sighed. "Nothing makes any sense."

"Come in, Max," she said firmly. "Just come in."

Directly inside their third-floor apartment was a narrow hallway, and then a living room, so crowded with objects that it seemed more like a series of individual cozy nooks than a single large room. There were a couple of old couches, and fat, comfortable-looking chairs with lamps on little tables next to them. Edges of faded oriental rugs peeked out from underneath the furniture. Bookcases lined the walls, and magazines were piled high on the tables beside various clocks and figurines. It had clearly taken them years of living here to amass this collection of stuff. I thought of the bright, empty house of this morning as I followed the girl into the kitchen.

This room was relatively uncluttered, with an old wooden table in the center. In a big bowl on the counter I noticed the remains of a salad consisting of bean sprouts, broccoli and tofu. There was a cabbagy smell.

"Sit down, Max," she said. "Do you want something to eat?"

"I don't want to eat. I just want to find out what's going on," I said, taking the chair she indicated.

She sat down across from me, leaning forward with her elbows on the table, slumping slightly. The girl I met this morning didn't slump. Though their features were identical, I began to notice that there were other differences between them, beside the superficial ones of clothing and hairstyle. This one was softer, a little fleshier.

"Yes, I'm sure you do want to know what's going on," she said, pushing back a stray strand of hair. "It must be driving you crazy, somebody as nose—I mean as inquisitive as you are."

"What do you mean?"

"Don't you remember how flustered Dad got yesterday when you wouldn't stop asking him questions about his work?" She smiled slightly. "But he was also pretty impressed when you started rattling off the equations from his paper."

I sat up quickly. "You know I read his paper? But you couldn't know that, unless I really *did* meet you at the labs yesterday! You really *must* be the right ones!"

She looked puzzled. "Of course we are," she said, as though it should be completely obvious to me.

I sank back in the chair, relieved. "If you only knew how good it feels, to finally know something for sure. So tell me, what else happened at the labs yesterday?"

But now she looked worried. "You really believed the others were us? What did they ask you? How much did you tell them?"

I'd thought I was about to learn something, and she just went on asking me questions. "Yes, I thought they were the real Sylvans! What else was I supposed to think? And when are you going to tell me what's going on? You said you would. Who *are* those people, anyway? Why do you want that thing, whatever it is? And what happened to me at the labs yesterday?"

"How much do you remember?"

"Nothing. All I remember is going to bed the night before the tour, and waking up this morning. Are you going to tell me or not?"

"You don't remember going to the labs? At all? You don't remember anything that happened before my father . . ." She left the sentence hanging.

"Now *you're* doing it too!" I stood abruptly and paced a few steps. The kitchen, I saw now, was stocked with jars of seeds and whole grains and other health foods, and on the refrigerator door was a chart labeled THE ANTI-CANCER DIET. I turned back to her. "Why can't you tell me what's going on? Why can't anybody understand how *I* feel? First I lose a whole day, then all this craziness starts. How do you expect me to help you if I don't know what's happening?"

"I'm not supposed to tell you. My father has to. At least we know it's safe from them in your jacket at the cleaners. They'll never find it there. You have no idea how dangerous they are."

I paced again, to avoid looking at her, more worried than angry now. How was I going to tell her that the object *wasn't* safe at the cleaners but was here in their apartment, where the people I met could easily find it? They could show up at any minute. Were they really dangerous? I faced her again. "Do they know where you live?"

She nodded. "They must. And they were probably following you."

"I don't think so; I was watching for their car. And I think they believed me when I said I didn't take anything from the labs."

"I hope so."

The kitchen door opened. A man in a wrinkled whitish shirt and gray polyester pants entered the room. His hair was long and unkempt, he had a protruding belly and a slightly dazed expression. But in every other respect he was the twin of the man on the trampoline. Again, I felt a shock of dreamlike unreality. "Why do they look . . . so much like both of you?" I said, staring at him.

He didn't seem to hear me. "Did he tell them anything?" he said anxiously to Eve. His manner was rather timid, his faced lined and a little jowly; he was clearly no athlete. Yet there was no doubt that he was genetically the same person as the man I had met this morning.

"He says he didn't."

He nodded and sank into a chair. "Good. I thought he'd work out."

"You thought I'd work out?" I didn't like being talked about as though I were an object. "What do you mean? What could I tell them, anyway?"

The man looked questioningly at Eve. "He seems to have forgotten the whole day," she told him. "Even what happened before you gave it to him."

The man groaned and put his hand to his forehead. "Oh, God, I must have overdosed him. What's wrong with me? We really *are* lucky they didn't get anything out of him—if it's true."

"Overdosed?" I said, my voice rising. "What do you mean by that?"

The man closed his eyes and sighed deeply. Eve looked away from me, playing with the end of her braid.

"Overdosed?" I said again, hardly able to believe what I was hearing. I sat down slowly. "Is *that* why I have amnesia, why I left the labs early? Because you drugged me?"

Eve leaned toward me. Her face was blander than the other one's, without the emphasis of makeup. But now her expression seemed pained, and her eyes met mine as though she might actually be concerned about me. "Try to understand, Max. It all happened so fast. We had no time to plan very well. We had to hide it someplace they would never suspect."

"Such as my jacket pocket," I said, amazed. "Safe from them at the cleaners. But . . . how did you know Mom would take it to the cleaners?"

"That was Eve's idea," Sylvan said. "The kind of detail I wouldn't have thought of. Spill oil on the sleeve, she said, and his mother would take it to the cleaners right away."

"Yes, but . . . but to *drug* me? Why didn't you just *tell* me what was going on?"

"We couldn't," Eve said. "If they found you, and you knew, they would have forced you to tell them. And they *did* find you, and you *would* have told them this morning, if you'd known." She reached for my arm, pleading with me to understand. "And we just *couldn't* let them get it, Max."

I pushed her hand away. "But you *could* slip me some dangerous drug that erased my memory. You used me. You overdosed me, you could have poisoned me, and you're still not telling me *why!*" I banged my fist so hard on the table that the bottles of vitamin pills jumped, then pushed back my chair and stood up. I was furious and hurt and confused, and didn't know what to do. I had to think about it by myself. I started for the door.

"Did you get the receipt?" the man asked Eve.

"Max, wait," she said. "You never gave me the—"

"Right, the receipt," I said, turning back from the door. I had forgotten all about it. "Okay." I paused, thinking. "If you want me to give it to you, you're going to have to tell me what's going on. I *have* to know."

Eve looked from me to her father. "You don't want to know," he said. "You'll be safer if you don't. We'll all be safer."

"Tell me," I insisted. "I'm part of it now. You *made* me part of it. Otherwise, *I* keep the receipt."

Sylvan pulled nervously at his long hair and then cleared his throat. "Eve, I guess you'd better go get that manuscript of . . . of my latest paper, the one I decided not to publish," he said reluctantly. "It's on my desk."

"Are you sure you should show him?"

"Yes, he's sure," I told her.

"Go get it, Eve," he said, looking down at the table. "After what we did to him he . . . he deserves some kind of explanation."

She sighed, and slowly left the room.

Sylvan faced me directly for the first time. "Those people look like us because . . . they *are* us."

I sat down again, watching him skeptically. "What's *that* supposed to mean?"

He stared at the tabletop. "The timeline they came from

must have been very much like ours. They are our equivalents there. Or anyway, they *were*, before . . ."

"Before *what?*" I prodded him.

He sighed. "It's so difficult for a nonscientist to understand."

"I understood those equations in your other paper, remember?" I told him. "Just go on."

Eve returned and put the paper on the table, a few Xeroxed sheets stapled together. "Universal Bifurcation to Chaos as a Function of Nonlinear Temporal Displacement," read the title. Sylvan stared down at it. "I thought it was only theoretical, at first. There was a part of me that refused to believe I could actually implement it physically. And then I . . . I *did* do it." He breathed in sharply, as though he was about to cry. "Such a *little* mistake, such a minor miscalculation. And the consequences!"

Eve put one hand on his shoulder. "Dad, you've blamed yourself enough."

"What kind of mistake?"

"Dad, are you sure you should—" Eve started to caution him.

But Sylvan obviously needed to get something off his chest. "When I first tested the phaser, I accidentally sent a specimen back, instead of forward. And that's what generated the first bifurcation, that's what finally resulted in the timeline they came from. And then they must have made other bifurcations, lots of them." He shook his head. "A mistake of only a few seconds—and then chaos. Sensitive dependence on initial conditions. *So* sensitive . . ."

36

I was having trouble understanding him. What did he mean about sending something back instead of forward? But there was one concept that was familiar to me. "Bifurcation?" I said, remembering something. "Let me see that." I pulled the paper away from him. I quickly scanned the beginning, equations similar to the ones I'd seen before, then flipped it over to the second page. Figure 1 leapt out at me. It was a little startling to see it again. But this time it did not give me the dizzy sensation I had felt when I saw it this morning.

I lifted my eyes from it and looked at Sylvan. "He had this same graph on his wall, a great big one," I said. "And he seemed to *know* it would give me that horrible feeling, before I even told him."

"What horrible feeling?" Sylvan said instantly.

"That I was falling into it. That I'd been there before— like a kind of *déjà vu*, sickening, but also . . . a little exciting."

Sylvan's expression sharpened. "Then what did he say?"

I tried to remember. "Nothing. That was when the phone rang. After that, we stopped talking about the graph."

"Did it give you this . . . this awful feeling just now?"

I shook my head. "No. This time it just looked familiar. Maybe his had that weird effect on me because it was so much bigger."

"No, that's not the reason. It did that to you because you were with *them*."

"What difference would that make?"

"They're functioning as strange attractors now, obviously."

Now I was really confused. "But strange attractors are mathematical things that drag systems into chaos. How can *people* be strange attractors?"

"In their own timeline, their own universe, they were just people. But now they're in *our* universe—and they don't belong in it," Sylvan explained. "They've been in chaos, they probably *created* chaos in their timeline by doing something insane, such as playing the stock market with the phaser. And then they wanted to get out of chaos, to someplace safe, and somehow they managed to find their way here, to a stable timeline. And now they want to insert themselves into this timeline. And in order to do that, they have to get rid of us and take our places here." His jowls trembled. "And if they ever *do* get their hands on my phaser, they'll drag *this* timeline into chaos too!"

I started to ask him what the phaser was. Then I knew it had to be the thing in my protopack. "But what does this thing they want—the phaser, you call it?—have to do with the graph? What does the phaser do, anyway?"

"I've told you enough," Sylvan said wearily. "All you need to know is how dangerous those people are, and how disastrous it would be if they got the phaser. The more information you have, the more vulnerable you'll be. Just give me the receipt and go home."

"But what if they followed him here?" Eve said. This one was quieter, steadier than the Eve from this morning, but she was certainly alert. "What if they question him?

He knows where the phaser is now. Can we trust him?"

"We can only hope they thought he really was ignorant, that he was the wrong student, that we planted it on somebody else. Then they'll be tracing some of the others."

"But what . . ." Eve looked at me. "Of course, you didn't tell them you had amnesia, did you?"

"What do you mean? Sure I told them."

"Then they *do* know it's him," Sylvan said in a tragic whisper.

"But what did you *expect* me to do?" I protested. "I didn't know I wasn't supposed to tell them I had amnesia! And it was the truth."

"It's my fault," Sylvan said, surprising me. "I drugged him so that he wouldn't know anything, wouldn't give anything away. But I didn't think ahead enough to see that amnesia would also make them suspect him."

Eve reached out to try to comfort him again. They both seemed so hopeless now that I felt sympathy for them, despite what they had done to me. "But they really *did* seem to believe I didn't know anything about it, when I left," I said. "If they thought I was the one they should be after, do you think they would have let me go so easily?"

"Maybe . . . maybe he's right," Sylvan said, brightening a little. "Maybe they don't suspect him anymore, and we have a chance. But you better go now, Max, while you're still safe."

"You're really not going to tell me anything else?"

"If I do, we'll all just be more vulnerable if they ever get their hands on you again," he said, not unreasonably.

"But if this phaser thing is so important, so dangerous, why didn't you get Security at the labs to hide it instead of planting it on me?"

"Because I couldn't let *anyone* know it even existed; it was too dangerous. Anyway, they had already infiltrated Security, bribed somebody. Someone had been going through my lab; someone who had security access. One of the guards downstairs even made a remark about seeing my twin brother. That's how I knew they were around. It happened so fast. I had to hide it—and then your group came along." He shook his head and looked away from me. "Go home. Stay there. Lock the doors. Don't answer the phone."

That's all he was going to tell me. Tired and worried as he seemed, I could sense his implacable stubbornness.

"The receipt," Eve murmured.

I gave him the receipt. It was useless now, of course, because the phaser wasn't at the cleaners, it was in my protopack.

Something was preventing me from giving him the phaser. I told myself that it was safer with me than with him. He was the one the others were really after, the one they knew it belonged to, the one they would logically be following. He had also made several very big blunders with it and might blunder again. I was younger, more alert, more competent. It was safer hidden with me.

But there was another part of me that knew I was probably making a terrible mistake, that keeping it was worse than any lie. And yet, for the first time in my life, I was able to ignore this inner voice. Because I didn't want to give up the phaser. I just couldn't do it. It was crazy—just as crazy as the fact that I still wanted to see the other Eve again, even knowing that I could never see her, because it would be too dangerous.

I was very edgy when Eve saw me to the apartment door, and it must have shown. "Be careful, Max. I'm worried about you," was the last thing she said to me, and I believed she meant it, in a way I somehow didn't believe the other Eve. And yet, in the car, I stopped thinking about *this* Eve almost immediately.

I thought about the phaser. I tried to put together all the hints Sylvan had given me. I wondered about the keys labeled DEPARTURE TIME and ARRIVAL TIME. What could they mean? What could the phaser have to do with the bifurcation graph, and this other universe Sylvan was talking about? I remembered what I had read about time travel, and changing the past, a favorite daydream of mine. I thought about quantum mechanics and its theory of multiple universes. By the time I reached my neighborhood, I was beginning to come up with an explanation. It was pretty fantastic—but not that much more fantastic than running into two versions of the same two people. More than anything else, the explanation was scary.

The more I thought about it, the more nervous I was. If Sylvan was right, then the object in my protopack was more valuable and destructive than *any* nuclear device, and here I was carrying it, with no protection at all.

Almost as frightening was the fact that something I didn't understand had instinctively made me hold onto it. What did that mean? I'd be safe if I hadn't kept it; now I was in danger. I remembered the list of students I'd seen this morning; the others had obviously filched it from the labs. Was the phone call they hadn't wanted me to hear a report from one of Sylvan's spies there? If he could get through Mercury Labs' Security so easily, what chance did I have?

I was so terrified and jittery when I got close to home that I stopped the car about a half block before the turnoff onto our dead-end street. I got out of the car and crept toward the corner, trying to keep hidden behind trees and shrubbery.

And just around the corner, waiting behind the stone gatepost at the entrance to our street, where I wouldn't have seen it until it was too late, was the silver Jeep Cherokee.

6

I ran to the car, backed it up all the way to the corner, and turned right onto another street.

They knew I had the phaser—otherwise they'd be at Eve and Sylvan's, not waiting for me here. Sylvan's whole plan of hiding the phaser from them had failed. And it was all my fault. If only I'd left it at the cleaners!

But now maybe I could fix things up.

I parked the car a couple of blocks from home, then took the phaser out of the protopack and stared at it, remembering Sylvan's equations and everything I'd read about time travel.

Changing the past is the big problem with time travel. Let's say you went into the past and accidentally killed your father when he was a boy. Then you never would have been born. But if you had never been born, how could you go into the past and accidentally kill your father? It's an impossible paradox.

Unless you turn to quantum mechanics, and the theory of multiple universes, or timelines. According to this way of thinking, when you change the past the timeline splits, or bifurcates. Now there are two timelines, one in which your father died as a boy, and another in which he lived and had children. I thought of the title of Sylvan's paper: "Universal Bifurcation to Chaos as a Function of Nonlinear Temporal Displacement." Or, to put it in layman's terms: "Timelines Splitting Apart as a Result of Changing the Past—Ending in Chaos."

Did the lines on the graph represent multiple universes? Was the phaser a time machine? And if it was, could I use it to slip past the others?

I took a mechanical pencil out of the protopack. I switched on the phaser and touched the pencil to the Velcro-like strip. *New Specimen: 16.1. Enter* DEPARTURE TIME read the display.

I entered a departure time of one minute. I started to enter an arrival time of two minutes earlier. But I stopped myself in time. If I did that, then another pencil should have appeared two minutes ago, and that hadn't happened. If I sent the pencil into the past, I would be changing the past, generating another universe in which the pencil *had* appeared two minutes ago—making a bifurcation.

44

That was exactly the mistake Sylvan had made. He sent something into the past, and suddenly another universe existed, with another Sylvan and another phaser. And that Sylvan made *more* bifurcations. The graph expanded dizzily in my mind, timelines doubling and sprouting, rushing faster and faster out of control like some monstrous grasping plant in a speeded-up film. And at the end, the infinite jungle of chaos.

It hit me then, with full force, how disastrous it was to make bifurcations. That was why the phaser was so dangerous, why changing the past was the worst thing anyone could do. Every change in the past made a bifurcation, and every bifurcation brought the timelines closer to chaos.

I took a couple of deep breaths, trying to think logically. I still had to slip by the others. And now that I had started this experiment with the phaser, I somehow couldn't stop. I told myself that sending the pencil into the future couldn't make a bifurcation; it wouldn't be changing the past in any way. I thought it through again, carefully, then entered an arrival time two minutes from now. I put the pencil down on the seat next to me. I pressed ACTIVATE and watched the pencil.

In one minute the phaser beeped. The pencil vanished.

I held my breath. Was this really happening? I kept my eyes on the spot where the pencil had been. A minute later the phaser beeped again. The pencil reappeared.

I picked it up. It was the same pencil, undamaged, no different from before in any way that I could tell. I closed my eyes and opened them again.

"This thing really *is* a time machine," I whispered. I

punched myself in the head. Goose bumps raced across my arms. Then I was bouncing up and down on the seat, laughing idiotically.

It took me a few minutes to pull myself together. Okay, so it was a time machine. But what you could safely do with it was very limited. You couldn't go into the past, because then you might change the past, making a bifurcation, which would lead to chaos. It also meant that if you went into the future, you couldn't come back—coming back from the future meant going into the past, risking a bifurcation. So all you could do with it was travel very short distances into the future, short enough so that you wouldn't have to return, but could wait for the past to catch up with you.

But maybe I could still use it to get by the others. How long were they going to wait there, anyway? Why couldn't I just move ahead bit by bit until they were gone? I drove slowly to a spot a block and a half away from where the Jeep Cherokee was waiting and parked. I could just see the top edge of the Jeep's silver roof, sticking up above the stone wall at the right side of our street.

Was it safe to use the phaser on myself? It didn't seem to have hurt the pencil, but that was only an inanimate object. Could a human body withstand the stress of temporal displacement?

The others seemed perfectly healthy, and they must have used one to get into our universe, if what Sylvan said this afternoon was true. And was it also true that they would drag us into chaos if they got this phaser? And if they had their own—which they must have used to get here—then why did they want this one? There was a lot I didn't understand, but I knew I couldn't let them get it away from me. I had to sneak by them.

I touched the rough surface, feeling a slight electric shock. *Specimen 15.1* appeared on the display. I punched in a departure time of one minute, and an arrival time eleven minutes from now. They probably wouldn't be gone after only ten minutes, but I wanted to be careful at first and not send myself very far. What I was doing was already risky enough.

I pressed ACTIVATE. The minute seemed to go on forever. What was it going to feel like? Was it too late to stop it now?

The phaser beeped.

At first I thought it hadn't worked, since I felt nothing at all. My watch was still telling the same time as before. But the clock on the phaser was now ten minutes ahead of where it had been. And when I checked the rearview mirror I saw that the car that had been parked behind me was gone. Next time I'd look out the window, not at the phaser. It would be interesting to see the instant changes. I set the phaser to send me ahead twenty minutes and pressed ACTIVATE.

Shadows jumped, leaves flickered into another position, a couple of cars vanished and a couple of new ones appeared. A woman and a dog materialized across the street. "*Amazing*," I murmured, grinning. And then I noticed that the roof of the Jeep Cherokee was no longer glinting behind the stone wall. They were gone.

"That was easy," I congratulated myself. I sank back

against the seat, my eyes closing, suddenly aware of how tense I had been. But I didn't sit there for long; I was eager to get home. I set my watch a half hour ahead, to the time on the phaser, thinking about what I should do next. I got by them this time, but I was still going to have to be very careful. They would be back. I zipped the phaser into the protopack. I was going to have to find a really good hiding place for it, something foolproof. I turned the key in the ignition, briefly glancing in the rearview mirror to see if time travel had made me look any different. The Jeep Cherokee was parked a block behind me on the other side of the street.

"No!" I said, panicking. What were they doing there? Maybe they'd noticed my car, and saw that it was empty—I'd just been away for twenty minutes—and were waiting for me to come back and get it. I couldn't let them see me. I got out the phaser and rapidly pushed buttons to jump a half hour into the future. I pressed ACTIVATE. Leaves blinked, shadows leapt out like living things, the sky darkened toward evening. And the Jeep Cherokee jumped half a block closer.

I phased ahead another half hour, not knowing what else to do. The car in front of me instantly expanded to become the Jeep, facing me, its bumper inches from mine. Eve and Sylvan were inside, their eyes on me, laughing. Before I could think, they jumped out of the car.

I pulled my Swiss Army knife out of the protopack and shoved it in my pocket, dropped the phaser into the protopack and zipped it shut, which didn't give me time to lock the doors or roll up the window. Eve pulled open the passenger door and slid in. Sylvan poked his head through the window beside me, leaning casually against the car, grinning.

"Welcome to the club, Max," he said. I smelled liquor on his breath.

"Leave me alone! Get away from me!" I shouted.

"Oh, come on, Max. I can't believe you like *them* better than *us*," Eve said, so close beside me that her hair brushed my ear.

"You're wasting your time. I don't have it!" I said pointlessly, knowing they had just seen me appear out of nowhere.

"That's okay, Max. You can ride with us," Sylvan said. Something rough touched my cheek; I felt a slight electric shock.

I jerked away from the sensation, at the same time reaching out to try to grab his phaser. But he already had it out of reach, holding it above his head with one hand. "You'll *love* the year 33,019 B.C., Max," he said eagerly, still smiling. "That's where our adventures start. We have a special hideout there. We can get to it from our house. Come on, let's go!"

"You can't do this!" I yelled.

"You're registered on my phaser now," Sylvan pointed out. "If you don't come quietly, like a good boy, I can send you even farther into the past—4.5 billion years, for instance, to the molten earth. It's rather warm there."

"Oh, Max, relax. We'll have fun at the hideout," Eve coaxed me. "You can't get away from us anyway."

She was right. I couldn't.

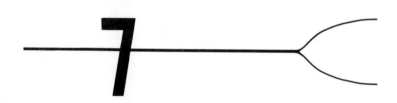

I tried to resist at first, refusing to budge from my car. Sylvan clamped his hand around my neck, hard, and thrust his phaser in front of my eyes. On the display I could clearly see the arrival time of 4.5 billion years ago. "I'll do it, Max, believe me," he said.

"He will, Max," Eve whispered. "Don't make him."

I couldn't turn my head, but I slid my eyes toward her. She looked quickly from Sylvan back to me. "Please, Max, just come with us. No one's going to hurt you, I promise," she said.

What choice did I have? Sylvan drove the jeep fast, gesturing with his phaser, babbling about incredible adventures in the past.

But I didn't believe in any hideout in the year 33,019 B.C. All Sylvan really wanted was the phaser. Once he got me to the waterfall house, where I couldn't get help, he would just beat me up and take the phaser. I might have considered jumping out at a stoplight, except that all the doors were locked, under Sylvan's control. I sat stiffly in the backseat, terrified, unable to think. All I knew was that if he brought this timeline into chaos, it would be my fault.

But when he parked in the space outlined in white in front of the concrete house, he didn't move to get out of the car. Leaving the motor running, he pushed buttons on the phaser. "Get ready, here we go!" he called out. Eve turned around in the front seat, grinning at me, her face vivid with makeup.

"Wait a minute! What are you—" I started to say.

Sylvan pressed ACTIVATE. The phaser beeped.

The house, the trees, the hillside vanished. The earth dropped away. We landed with a slight bounce on a large platform at the top of a crude wooden ramp, which sloped about one story down to the ground. Sylvan gunned the motor and zoomed to the bottom of the ramp, then bumped away across the plain that stretched emptily to the horizon in all directions. There were no roads for him to follow, but he made frequent turns, sending up dirt as he spun the car around.

"I set up this hideout back here for a reason, of course,"

he bragged. "The Siberians won't cross over the Bering Strait from Asia for fifteen thousand years. There's nobody on this continent. Not to mention, this happens to be an interglacial period in the middle of the last Ice Age, a brief thaw. Before any humans *do* get here, the glaciers will have come back and pulverized whatever's left of the hideout. The whole place is made of biodegradable materials from the future. It won't even end up as a fossil, let alone a bifurcation."

Was it possible that he *wasn't* kidding, and we really *were* in 33,019 B.C.? I stared out the window, my heart pounding. It was nightmarish to look around and see nothing but endless grassland—no buildings, no trees. I turned and looked out the back, but I could no longer see the ramp. Sylvan's frequent turns had taken away my sense of where it had been, and in the gathering dusk I would never be able to find it on my own. I had never felt so far away from home, or so trapped.

But I still had the phaser. I couldn't get out of the car, but maybe I could use it to get back from *inside* the jeep.

"I wouldn't try using your phaser to get home," Sylvan told me, as if he had just read my mind. "The earth is a lot lower here, obviously, so you'd end up implanted in somebody's lawn, or inside some object. You'd be blown to bits. Things are empty in 33,019 B.C., so we can get here fast without worrying about landing inside something else. But the world is crowded where we come from. Getting back is a lot trickier."

The landscape certainly looked prehistoric. Assuming we really were as far back in the past as he claimed, it made sense that the earth would be lower. And I knew that the parking place in front of their house was at the same level as the top of the ramp. But now, even if I could get out of the car, I wouldn't be able to find the ramp. It began to sink in that I really couldn't use the phaser to get back, without killing myself.

And as soon as we got to their hideout, Sylvan would take the phaser away from me. Then I wouldn't be able to do anything at all. But I still had the Army knife. I swore to myself that I would use it, as soon as Sylvan tried to get the phaser.

I kept staring out at the bleak evening landscape. As helpless and terrified as I felt, I was also aware of a prickling of excitement. We really *must* have gone back thousands of years. This was time travel; it was actually happening to me! And if all Sylvan wanted from me was the phaser, why had he bothered to take me here, instead of just getting the phaser away from me back at home? Was it possible, as he had hinted, that they really were taking me on some kind of adventure?

"Where are we going, anyway?" I asked Sylvan. "Why is this hideout so far away? Why didn't you just put it at the bottom of the ramp?"

He laughed. "You haven't figured it out yet? You seem smart enough to appreciate the logic of it. I put the hideout in the same space occupied by the basement of the other Sylvan's apartment house in the twentieth century. That's convenient for me, for a lot of reasons."

The hideout turned out to be a luxurious mobile home. It was quite large, but probably not too large to have been pulled here by the powerful jeep. The picture window, shiny white siding, and futuristic generator were startlingly incongruous in the middle of this treeless barren wilderness. The silence, when Sylvan turned off the motor, sank down on us like a vast ocean of velvet.

Sylvan pressed a button and the door locks clicked open. They both hopped out of the car, making no move to attack me, and began purposefully unloading provisions from the back—cartons of liquor and soft drinks, bags of groceries.

I waited in the car, crouching a little, but they continued to ignore me. Finally I stepped cautiously outside. The air was chilly, though it was almost midsummer, and the stars, beginning to appear, seemed amazingly bright.

Eve glanced up at me from the back of the jeep. It was almost too dark to see now, but I caught the flash of her teeth as she smiled, her hair a faint tangle of silver against the sky. "Well? Are you just going to stand there and let us do all the work?" She lifted a plastic shopping bag.

She sounded as though we had just come back from a routine trip to the supermarket. Did they think I was going to forget that they had kidnapped me? "How long are you going to keep me here?" I demanded.

"That's up to you, Max," Sylvan said. He was in no position to attack me, balancing a carton of liquor on his shoulder. He must have slipped the phaser into the yellow pack he still wore around his waist. "If you cooperate, I can get you back only a couple of seconds after we left. You won't be late, your parents won't worry for a minute. Usually we don't do that—we stay in the same time frame, here and in the twentieth century. If we stay here for five hours, we go back five hours after we left. It keeps things simpler, and prevents jet lag. But I can always make exceptions. Stick with us and you'll find out more." He turned away from me, kicked open the door of the mobile home, and stepped inside.

I was baffled. Why wasn't he trying to take my phaser? "But aren't you going to . . ." I started to say.

"Can't you ever calm down, Max?" Eve said. "Help us get this stuff inside and then *please* try to relax. We're going to have a super evening." A light went on inside the mobile home, illuminating half of her face, and I caught the excitement in her eye. She turned away. "Now are you going to help us with this stuff or not?"

I didn't see any alternative. I was just as trapped outside the house as I would be inside it. I couldn't get back to my own time—and there was no place else to go in 33,019 B.C.

When we had finished unloading, Sylvan got us each an ice cold beer—it was warm inside the mobile home. He sat me down in a comfortable chair in the living room, lit a cigarette, and lounged across from me on a white canvas couch, handsome in a blue polo shirt and khaki shorts. He set his bare feet on the glass coffee table, beside an overflowing ashtray, and lifted his beer in a toast.

"As I said, Max, welcome to the club. You've used the phaser successfully; you're one of us now. I can share my knowledge with you. You won't believe the adventures we're going to have. And don't think that's an empty promise. I'm talking about tonight."

"Yes, Max, welcome," Eve said, coming in from the kitchen. She smiled down at me so infectiously that, despite my tension, I couldn't help smiling back. She stood there for a moment, then set a plate of what looked like deep-fried pork rinds on the coffee table and moved toward the door. "Let me know if you need anything; I'll be fixing dinner."

Sylvan leaned forward and shoved a handful of the rinds into his mouth. "Have some, Max, they're great," he mumbled, his cheeks bulging.

I was beginning to notice how hungry I was, and tried one, tentatively. To my surprise, it was not at all disgusting. I helped myself to a handful.

"So what do you want to know, Max? How to play the market with the phaser? I'll tell you all the tricks. I made a lot of money that way."

"I bet you also made a lot of bifurcations."

He shrugged, and took a swig of beer.

I couldn't get over how casual he was about using the phaser. He seemed so sure of himself. Was it possible that you *could* use it safely? I remembered the graph, sweeping out and spreading malevolently across the timelines, bringing disaster. And this guy merely shrugged it off! His blandness about the destructive power in his hands was unsettling, almost irrational. The other Sylvan's cringing apprehensiveness was a lot easier to understand.

"Oh, I see, you've been listening to *him*," Sylvan said, once again seeming to read my mind. "Believe me, he's ignorant, a fool." He blew out a quick puff of smoke, then went on with contempt in his voice. "He has no on-site experience. But I've *been* to chaos, and back. Think about that, Max. I'm telling you, it can be done.''

Again I felt the prickling of excitement, a crazy desire to get a look at chaos. It was the same feeling I've sometimes had when standing on the top of a cliff, a perverse kind of temptation to step over the edge. But I tried to ignore it, thinking again of the graph. This Sylvan was frightening, but his attitude also made me angry. ''So you went around doing anything you wanted, cheating the stock market, piling up money, making bifurcations left and right,'' I said. ''And then when you had enough, you just left the mess you had made and came over to our universe. And now you want to get rid of the other Eve and Sylvan, and take their places here. Is that it?''

He kept his feet on the table, lighting a new cigarette. ''What do you mean, *your* universe? We came back to where we started from, before all the bifurcations. And now that I've got what I need, I am certainly *not* going to generate another bifurcation, for any reason.'' He spread his hands, balancing his cigarette between two fingers. The smoke slid up into the air in a straight line, then suddenly dispersed. ''Don't fall for that impostor's lies. *They're* the ones who don't belong here, not us.''

He spoke with conviction, and I almost wished I could believe him. Even though this Sylvan's use of the phaser was reckless, even though all the evidence indicated that these two were the impostors, they were so much more interesting than the others. And more open too, now that they knew I had the phaser. Sylvan had volunteered to share his knowledge with me.

57

From the kitchen, I could hear Eve humming along softly to a tape, cooking something that was beginning to smell very delicious. I wondered what Eve felt about her father's risky behavior with the phaser. Did she go along with him because she wanted to, or because he forced her? When she had warned me that Sylvan would indeed send me back 4.5 billion years, she seemed afraid of him. Now both of them were relaxed and friendly, not threatening in the least, trying to create a pleasant evening for me, a party. And what was this exciting adventure Sylvan had in mind for later in the evening? Maybe I should let my guard down and try to enjoy what was happening.

And then it hit me again—I was Sylvan's prisoner. The fact that I could forget I was trapped only made the prison more insidious and inescapable. There was no need for him to do anything crude such as tying me up; I was registered on his phaser. He couldn't move me through space, but that didn't matter. If I tried to escape headlong into the future, risking suicide, Sylvan could instantly bring me back to this time. And if I ever got on his nerves, he could take my phaser away from me and send me 4.5 billion years into the past. I didn't doubt that he would do it. Anyone who would throw a timeline into chaos, just to make money—and then leave the destroyed universe behind him—would have no qualms about killing a single individual.

I watched him popping pork rinds into his mouth, smacking his lips, and suddenly had to look away, panic rising in my gut. If he had shown only a trace of anxiety or doubt he would have been a lot less disturbing. It was his simple pleasure in manipulating the universes that made his joviality so sinister. Would I ever understand him? I wondered, again, if being registered on his phaser meant I would never be able to get away from him.

And when was he going to try to take the phaser away from me? He hadn't made a move so far. But when he did, I didn't realistically see any way I'd be able to keep him from getting it.

"Time to eat," Eve called from the kitchen.

"Maybe, if things work out, I might let you have a little peek at chaos yourself, Max," Sylvan suggested pleasantly, rising to his feet.

My mind kept switching back and forth. As inhuman as he had seemed a moment before, now I couldn't help but think that if *anybody* could show me chaos and get me out of it safely, it would be this guy, who had already been there and back. The other one couldn't offer me that. I pushed the graph out of my mind.

I'd never eaten a meal like this before. Each of us had an individual basket of strange gluey rice. I watched the others wad up balls of rice in their fingers and use them as edible scoops to dip into the common dishes of rich meats and seafood in the center of the table. But I didn't move to touch the food.

"Come on, Max. Dig in," Sylvan urged me. He gestured at the freshly opened bottle beside my plate. "And have another beer. It's the only thing to drink with this food."

"You can't blame me for being careful," I said. "Being drugged once was bad enough."

They exchanged a glance, but said nothing, continuing

to eat; obviously the food wasn't poisoned, and I was ravenous. I tentatively picked up a glob of the sticky rice, kneaded it between my fingers, and dipped it into a dish of something in a pinkish sauce. The seasoning was spicy-hot, producing an intense tingling sensation on my tongue. "This is *wonderful!*" I said, and gulped down some beer to cool my mouth. "Is this the way they eat in that other universe you came from?"

"Come off it, Max. You mean you've never been to Southeast Asia? You poor, deprived thing!" Eve said. "Don't believe those lies about us coming from another universe. I learned to cook this way from the hill tribes on the Thai-Laotian border. Bandits, some of them, but real sweethearts once you get to know them. Of course, I've changed the recipes slightly—I use a lot more meat and coconut cream, and not as many boring vegetables."

"We lived there for three months," Sylvan said. "We had to stay that long to really understand about opium. You can't just try it once and get sick, like the tourists."

"Don't you ever worry about what you're doing to your body?" I couldn't keep from asking him. "Getting addicted to opium? And smoking and drinking so much will kill you."

He shrugged. "Not me. All I have to do is go into the future and pick up a new pair of lungs or a fresh heart." He patted his trim waist. "And liposuction takes care of the gut." He popped an entire baby squid into his mouth, chewed it slowly, and added, "Speaking of substance abuse, what was that you said about being drugged?"

I was relaxed now. My head buzzed a little, probably because I wasn't used to drinking beer. "That's why I had

60

amnesia. Sylvan drugged me at the labs, but he gave me an overdose, so I forgot the whole day. He didn't want me to know they'd planted the—'' I gulped, and shoved a large piece of squid into my mouth, which was chewy enough to keep me out of the conversation for the moment.

"He *drugged* you?" Eve lifted her chin abruptly, a glob of dripping rice poised halfway to her mouth, and turned to her father. "God, talk about unscrupulous!" she said, sounding appalled. "They're more dangerous than we thought."

"Dangerous in more ways than one," Sylvan said softly. He turned to me, looking worried. "Be careful. That inept fool could have put you into a coma, Max. Maybe he *intended* to!" He shook his head. "I *knew* they were desperate, but I didn't know . . ." His voice faded.

"Okay, he drugged me. But they let me go right home," I pointed out. "They didn't kidnap me and hold me prisoner, like you."

"Did they explain things to you, and include you, like we have?" Sylvan asked me.

The other Sylvan had refused to tell me anything about the phaser. His excuse had been that knowing would make me more vulnerable.

"Well, Max?" Eve prodded me.

I struggled against giving in. I still had no reason to believe these two weren't just putting on a clever act. "But if the others are impostors, how come they were listed in the phone book? How come they were the ones I met at the lab? How come their apartment looked like they'd been there for years, and your house was empty?"

"I'm not denying the guy's name is Sylvan or that he works at the labs," Sylvan said smoothly. "But that doesn't prove the phaser belongs to him. I admit, I use the thing freely, I get a kick out of it. But I've learned from my mistakes—I know how to do it safely now. If I'd brought chaos to this timeline, you'd know it. I left a few little loose ends behind, that's all. We've been tracking them down. He's one of them. We had to try to get the phaser away from him before he made more mistakes with it and *really* caused some trouble. He knew we were out to get it from him, and he used you in a pitiful and dangerous attempt to hide it, which failed miserably." He leaned back in his chair and smiled and lit another cigarette. "I mean really, Max, which one of us is more on the ball, which one would *you* trust with it?"

I had to admit that he had just given me a logical explanation for why he wanted my phaser. He was beginning to seem more convincing—and certainly more competent—than the other Sylvan.

Then I thought of the old story about the sun and the wind trying to get the man to take off his coat. The wind's brute force only made the man wrap the coat more tightly around him; the sun's pleasant warmth did the trick. The enjoyable company they were offering me, the wonderful food, the promise of fantastic adventure, and especially the enticements Eve could provide in exchange for the phaser, were as persuasive as anything I could ever imagine. And he had just admitted that he wanted my phaser. That's why I still didn't trust this Sylvan. The fact that his goal was to get the phaser proved that everything he and Eve were doing was an act.

I pushed my chair away from the table. "Sorry, but I don't trust you. If you want the phaser, you'll have to take it—I won't give it to you."

They turned to each other, their faces blank. Then they looked slowly back to me. I got ready to leap out of the chair, feeling for the Swiss Army knife in my pocket. I was no match for Sylvan, but I'd go out fighting. It wasn't just that I didn't trust him; it also hurt me, almost physically, to think of parting with the phaser. I'd only used it a couple of times, but I already felt that it belonged to me, that it was part of me. I wouldn't give it up.

"But Max, I don't *want* it from you," Sylvan said.

"What?"

"I don't want your phaser, now that you've shown us what you're made of. I meant it when I said you're one of us now. You can keep it, if you help me just once."

"Keep it? But . . . but what do you want me to do?"

"It's trivial, Max," said Sylvan. "But, trivial as it is, you will be rewarded very handsomely. We'll give you a little taste beforehand, and after you do it—the adventures of the rest of your life will be the full reward. And I'll take your number off my phaser. Just a minor little favor for us, to earn your phaser, that's all I want. It's something you can do that we can't."

"Like what?" I demanded, belligerent because I was so confused. "What can I do that you can't?"

"Register the other Eve and Sylvan on the phaser," Sylvan said.

"What?" I jumped up from the table, staring at Sylvan. "You want me to register them? But . . ." I felt sick. "Then you'd have complete power over them, you could *kill* them!"

Sylvan watched me, his face expressionless. "It would make things a lot easier for me, Max," he pointed out. "They won't let either of us near them."

"What kind of a monster do you think I am?" I shouted. "I'd never do that in a million years! *You can't make me.*"

"Think about it, Max," Sylvan said, getting up and ambling into a room beyond the kitchen.

I turned to Eve, so shocked I didn't know what to say. "But . . ."

"Oh, Max, you shouldn't get so upset by him," she said lightly. "You're not going to let it ruin the whole evening, are you? Just forget it." She stood up and playfully flicked her napkin at me. "Don't *worry* about everything so much. Come on, help me with the dishes, so we can get started on our little expedition."

I helped her with the dishes, but I was still apprehensive. Why did Sylvan seem so unconcerned at my refusal to register the others? Did he think I would do it, despite my protest? Would he try to force me? And would he really let me keep my phaser if . . . But I refused to consider it. I tried to distract myself by speculating about this expedition they kept referring to.

Eve hummed softly to herself as we worked, utterly relaxed. Her calmness began to lull me. We didn't talk, but I couldn't ignore the pleasure I felt at being so close to her, so cozily domestic. Maybe I didn't need to worry about Sylvan so much.

Eve and I had just about finished when Sylvan came into the kitchen wearing nothing but a black and green skirt, wrapped around his waist, and his yellow pack. "Here, Max, put on your sarong," he said, offering me a piece of orange fabric. "I'll show you how to tie it. Don't worry, you can wear your pack. I won't try to take it from you."

"You expect me to dress like that? What for?"

"This is our surprise, Max." Eve's voice was husky with excitement. "You've never been to Southeast Asia. So we're taking you to Bangkok—*1910* Bangkok."

"What?" I almost dropped the plate I was drying. "Into the past?"

"Time travel, Max, the greatest adventure," Sylvan said softly, his eyes fixed on mine. "You know you want it."

"But . . . the past?" Was he really serious? "I mean, sure, time travel would be great. But why isn't the future good enough? Anyway, you *can't* go into the past. It would make a bifurcation."

"We're in the past now, Max."

"Yes, but there's nobody around here. You said yourself that's why you picked this place. If you went to a place like 1910 Bangkok, with other people and things around, it *would* make a bifurcation. It would bring on *chaos!*"

"Not if you do it right," Sylvan said, thrusting the garment at me. "Put it on, Max. You're coming with us— you don't have any choice. You're just slowing everything down by balking."

Eve changed in the back room. My hands trembled as I tied on the sarong, following Sylvan's instructions. I was scared. Going into the past was insanity. But I couldn't deny that part of me was also excited. And I didn't know of any way I could stop Sylvan from doing it.

I was especially aware of how silly I must look in the sarong when Eve appeared, more exotic than ever in a purple silk dress, cut high at the neck. But Sylvan gave me no time to feel embarrassed. He quickly took three objects that looked like flat, black life preservers out of a closet and ushered us outside. He tossed one to Eve and one to me. "Hoverpacks, Max. A trip like this requires flight. Watch how I put it on."

I shook my head, shivering in the cold June night air. This was all so crazy that I had just about given up trying to protest. I was also rapidly becoming more intrigued, and more curious. The thing fit snugly over my upper body like a vest and sealed itself by some invisible mechanism down the front. The power source across the back was amazingly small. "We can really fly in these things?" I asked Sylvan. "What makes them work, superconducting magnets?"

"Those were the granddaddies; technology progresses geometrically. This model was built in 2049."

I looked down at the hoverpack. The paper-thin control panel rested over my heart, consisting of colored bumps rather than keys. "You can practice here, in all this empty space, before we make the first jump," Sylvan said. Without warning he touched a bump on my control panel; my stomach dropped as the moonlit mobile home plunged away below us.

I thrashed wildly through the air like someone on the end of a gigantic bullwhip, punching the colored bumps and trying frantically not to lose the sarong. After about fifteen minutes I began to get the feel of the hoverpack. As soon as I had it more or less under control, I joined the others where they were waiting for me, floating several hundred feet over the prairie. Sylvan pulled out his phaser. He pressed the keys rapidly with one hand, hardly even looking at it: "2049, here we come," he said.

"We're jumping there from up here?"

"It's a lot safer to move around in time when you're airborne—you're less likely to land inside the middle of something. Anyway, I know what I'm doing." He checked an instrument on his wrist, led us fifteen feet higher, and rechecked the phaser. He lifted his finger to touch ACTIVATE.

"Wait!" I begged him. "How are we going to—"

His phaser beeped.

Light and noise exploded around us—and summer heat. We were hovering inches above the roof of a rainbow-glowing skyscraper, hidden from view by the protective shadow of a shell-shaped outcropping. Large candy-colored vehicles glided silently above us. Below, along the sides of the building, a labyrinth of moving walkways whizzed bored-looking people around at amazing speeds.

Fantastic as it was, I couldn't stop worrying. "Are you crazy? How are we going to get back without changing the past and making a bifurcation?"

"It's hard to change the past in the middle of the Great Plains in 33,019 B.C.," Eve explained. "You *know* that's why he picked it. All we have to be careful about is not bumping into ourselves on the way back." She squeezed my hand encouragingly.

"Or bumping into ourselves up here," Sylvan said, pointing. "But my timing is usually perfect. Look, there we go. . . . That sure was a fun trip."

Two figures in hoverpacks were zooming away from us, a man with red hair and a young woman in a purple jumpsuit. They disappeared quickly into the east, enclosed by a thirty-foot-wide cylindrical beam of light.

"That's . . . that's really you?" I murmured. "What's that kind of . . . of path you're following?"

"Hoverpack lanes; force fields. They protect hoverpack fliers from the vehicular traffic; try not to hit the boundary at high speed, though," Sylvan warned me.

The shimmering, silvery force fields, I saw now, radiated across the sky like pale, stationary klieg lights. Access to them was through a cylindrical portal on the roof of the building, blocked by an opaque barrier. We waited briefly in line, then Sylvan pressed his hand three times to a glowing blue panel to the left of the barrier—his handprint obviously functioned as a credit card. The barrier swirled open like a camera lens. We headed west, gaining speed, following the ascending silvery tunnel. It was transparent enough to allow us to see the lights of the neverending city, which were soon streaking away miles below us.

"It'll take us a couple of hours to get to Asia this way," Sylvan said. "But I thought you'd enjoy individual flight more than the instantaneous transport they have in the far future. And we have all the time in the world."

"Two hours to Asia? That means hypersonic speeds! But we *can't* be going that fast," I protested. "I don't feel any wind. And how can we be this high up without protection? I can breathe; I'm not even cold."

"The force field takes care of all that," Eve said, slipping her arm through mine.

It took me a while to get real control over my hoverpack. I kept losing my equilibrium at first and veering off at some unexpected angle, and we would have to struggle, clutching at each other, to get back together again. I also had problems with the sarong, which constantly threatened to unwrap itself from my waist. But gradually I got the hang of it all. And I began to enjoy myself—I just couldn't help it. Being so close to Eve while flying eight miles above the Pacific at Mach 10 was a pretty heady experience.

In what seemed like no time at all we were over the South China Sea. "What did I tell you, Max? Isn't this great?" Sylvan said, beaming at me. "I knew you'd finally loosen up and start having a good time."

"Yeah, it is pretty great," I had to admit. "As long as we don't make a bifurcation in 1910. Can't we just stay in the future?"

"But, Max, the past is the exciting part," Sylvan said, brimming with enthusiasm. "That's where the real challenge is. What you do in the future—buying things, interacting with people—doesn't really matter, because the future is still liquid, flowing, full of endless possibilities. Not much can go wrong there, and it's boring, Max. But not the past! How can I describe it?"

He looked down at the dark ocean, perfectly relaxed in his hoverpack, then gestured expansively with a cigarette. "The past is exquisitely fragile because it's frozen. You could say it's like a forest of delicate glass ornaments, all connected to one another, and you have to creep through it without brushing against a single thing. Or it's like . . . like an arrangement of millions of dominoes, balanced close beside one another. Knocking against just one of them will bring all the others crashing down. That's the thrill of it!"

"It scares the hell out of me," I said, meaning it.

"But I arranged this pleasure trip just for you. Wait until you see the details of how I constructed a bifurcation-proof window where we're headed," he tried to reassure me. "You're smart enough to appreciate it. That's the part I want to share with you—the painstaking process of it, the precisely detailed historical research, the delicate on-site covert investigation. You'll see. I spend most of my time on projects like this now."

Naturally we could not simply hire a long-tailed boat to cruise the Bangkok *klongs,* or canals. That would have required interaction with a native of past time, and exchange of money, small alterations of the past that could nevertheless multiply rapidly into universal bifurcations and chaos. Instead, Sylvan had located an abandoned though seaworthy boat which, at 11:01 P.M. on June 25, 1910, would come loose from its mooring on a deserted pier and drift away down the Chao Phrya River. We could use the boat until 1:26 A.M., when it would run aground near a temple, as long as we did not collide with any other vessels on the mostly deserted waterways, or attract any undo attention.

"But what if something happens and somebody in 1910 *does* see us?" I asked him. By this time we were drifting above the river in Bangkok in 2049. The muggy air was full of other hoverpack fliers, laughing, drinking, buying snacks from airborne food stalls. Eve and Sylvan were passing a joint back and forth, which they assured me was legal now.

"Look, no one's going to walk past that pier between

10 P.M. and 5 A.M. in 1910, I promise you, Max,'' Sylvan told me, exhaling smoke. ''And even if someone does happen to glimpse us in the boat, it won't create a bifurcation unless they see the hoverpacks.''

''How do you know? Maybe a little tiny change could make a bifurcation. Isn't just breathing *air* molecules in the past changing it?''

Sylvan waved the question away irritably. ''I've done it, Max, I've seen bifurcations happen. It takes a change of events on a human scale to make a bifurcation.''

''But why? Where do you draw the line? And what if we *do* bump into another boat on the river?''

Sylvan grimaced with impatience. ''I know what I'm doing!''

''Trust us, Max,'' Eve urged me. ''We'll be extra careful.''

I tried to believe her. We positioned ourselves carefully behind some palm trees so no one in Bangkok 2049 would see us vanish. Sylvan pressed keys, checked and double-checked the display. Eve took my hand. ''Here we go,'' Sylvan whispered. He lifted the phaser, breathing heavily, unable to suppress his quirky grin. He pressed ACTIVATE.

It was 10:50 P.M., June 25, 1910.

Electric lights vanished in the sudden silence; the moon blossomed over the river. I was almost too shaky to move, and let them guide me out onto the pier, above the lapping water, toward the sounds of a boat's creaking timbers. The river was low, the bedraggled boat five feet below the pier, but we managed to be nearly silent about climbing down into it.

It was a long, narrow boat, curving up at both ends with elaborately carved dragons, covered in the middle by a ragged canopy. There were no seats, only threadbare mats and carpets on the muddy floorboards. Eve and I moved to the bow, Sylvan remained at the stern. We took off our hoverpacks, just in case someone *did* see us, and at exactly 11:01 P.M. we floated away from the pier.

"But won't our weight make a difference in where the boat goes?" I whispered, turning gingerly back to Sylvan, afraid that anything I did might cause a bifurcation.

"Negligible," he said. "And I'll make sure we reach the temple at the right moment. I know exactly where it is. We'll be drifting with the current the whole time. All I have to do is nudge a little with the pole if our weight puts us slightly off course. But we don't even have to think about that for a while." He yawned. "I feel like taking a little snooze back here. You two enjoy the sights." His shadowy form sank down onto the mat at the stern of the boat.

I was still rigid with apprehension, aware that we were trespassers who could be disastrously caught at any moment. Eve calmly rolled up a carpet and arranged it to make a comfortable prop for our backs. She gestured for me to look around.

Drifting, the boat moved slowly into a narrow canal. I carefully moved my head to look. The tropical moon was full and very bright, clearly illuminating the banks of the dark brown *klong*. Wooden houses with steeply sloped, carved roofs sat on poles, all with porches and balconies and steps or ladders going down into the water. The utter uniqueness of what we were seeing, the privilege of being here, began to creep over me. Bangkok 1910 was a lively city; even at this time of night, charcoal braziers glowed on balconies and in windows. People sat on the porches, eating, drinking, singing. Many of them wore only sarongs.

I gazed at the people in amazement from the darkness of the boat, forgetting to worry now. We were actually in 1910! We could see wooden sewage pipes feeding into the filthy water, but naked children were bathing and swimming in it, women were washing clothes and dishes in it. There were palm and banana trees everywhere, and the gardens between and behind the houses were incredibly lush, rows of strange vegetables, also a profusion of flowers, and frequent large orchid gardens. We passed many beautiful temples, or *wats,* as Eve called them, brightly painted and carved with dragons. Beside every *wat* rose a stone pagoda.

It was like being in a dream—especially because of this affectionate girl sitting close beside me. She was as moved by what we were seeing as I was. I could sense it. And at a certain moment, quite naturally, I slipped my arm around her waist and kissed her. She kissed me back. It was the longest kiss of my life. I had never experienced anything like it.

We were interrupted by a rumble of thunder, and in the next instant the sky opened and we were immediately drenched, despite the canopy. Only now did I notice that the moonlight was gone; we could see nothing but the blurred pinpoints of braziers on the shore.

"That's the light we're heading for," Sylvan said behind us. "Over to the left there." His voice dropped to a whisper. "Quiet, now, don't want anybody to hear us." He began expertly maneuvering toward the light, the hissing clamor of the rain on the water covering the faint creak and splash of the boat.

"But if you knew when and where this boat was going to end up, you must have known it was going to rain too," I pointed out. "So how come you—"

"Shut up!" he ordered me, no longer cheerful.

"But if this was just supposed to be a pleasure trip, couldn't you have—"

"Shhh!" Eve hissed in my ear as she firmly clamped her hand over my mouth.

I pushed her hand away and peered ahead toward the flickering light. It illuminated a small section of bamboo pier, behind which loomed the tall, tapering black shape of a pagoda. As we swayed slowly closer, I saw that the light was a lantern, held by a bald man in a yellow robe. And then I noticed another boat, approaching the pier from the other direction, a lantern swinging in its bow. The man on the pier stepped toward it.

"Quick! Down on the floor," Sylvan ordered. "The lightning's coming in two seconds and this boat has to look empty."

I dropped to the floor with the others, too confused to argue. A tremendous burst of lightning forked across the entire sky. For an instant the river, pier, temple, and

75

pagoda were as bright as day. Carvings of grinning de-
mons leapt out at me. Another roll of thunder, louder
than the first, boomed overhead.

I didn't have a chance to be awed by Sylvan's perfect
timing, hiding us at exactly the moment when we might
have been seen, because in the next second Eve was
thrusting my hoverpack at me and we were all struggling
into them on the floor. Sylvan crawled past us to the bow,
pushing me aside roughly. Still stretched out on the floor,
he peered carefully up over the edge of the boat. The man
on the pier and the man in the other boat, which had
reached the pier, were staring directly at our boat now.
They spoke urgently to each other, arguing briefly, then
turned away from us, apparently convinced that our boat
was derelict, empty. The man on the pier produced a
small package from inside his robe.

Hidden by darkness again, Sylvan stood up with perfect
balance in the prow of our boat, poised inches from the
pier, his body tensed as though preparing to jump. I remembered him practicing on the trampoline; this kind of
adventure required agility. Eve moved silently past me to
the stern and picked up the pole.

I knew now that this was not a mere pleasure trip,
prepared for my benefit, but some horribly risky mission
of Sylvan's. Despite all of his talk about painstaking research and the details of constructing a bifurcation-free
window, he was about to interfere blatantly with the past.
Even the most minor interaction between him and these
two men, the slightest change in their lives, would multiply to create a gigantic bifurcation. And anything I did to

try to stop him would *also* create a bifurcation. I was terrified and furious, but I was also completely helpless. All I could do was watch, and hate him for what he was about to do.

And then he actually did it. He leapt onto the pier, grabbed the package from the two surprised men, and plunged back into the boat. Before he even hit the deck Eve was frantically poling the wildly rocking boat away from the pier. In an instant he was working beside her, while the two men were waving their arms and shouting after us.

"You're a *monster!*" I screamed, figuring it wouldn't make any difference now.

It didn't. Twenty feet behind us a gash of lightning struck the two men who had seen us. The water steamed as their bodies splashed into the canal.

Eve and Sylvan's cries of victory were almost buried by the third, and loudest, thunderclap. "Hurry, Max! People are already coming!" they urged me, rising into the air. In a moment they were practically invisible, fading into the rain and darkness. I followed them grimly back to the deserted pier where we had first found the boat. Crouching behind the same palm trees, we phased forward to 2049. We soared back to the trans-Pacific hoverpack lane and started for home.

They were triumphant, bursting with excitement, high on danger and success. "They were going to die anyway, Max. We changed nothing. There was no bifurcation," they both told me, many times, as we sped over the Pacific.

I didn't feel like talking. I thought of the dreamlike boat ride with Eve, hours that went by in minutes, and how quickly it dissolved into a nightmare. I thought of how I was trapped as a specimen on Sylvan's phaser, under his control, and how he wanted me to do the same thing to the other Eve and Sylvan. I was dazed, not knowing where I could go from here, what to do, feeling absolutely hopeless for the first time in my life. But finally, in response to their insistent urgings to cheer up and get it off my chest, I said, "Why? Why did you do it?"

"Why *not*, Max? What harm did we really do?"

"You interacted with the past. Something could have gone wrong. You could have made a bifurcation."

"But we didn't," Sylvan said. "You saw how careful I was."

Eve took my arm as the urban sprawl of Tahiti flashed below. "Why do you always have to concentrate on the bad parts?" she asked me. "I know you had as wonderful a time as I did. Think about that."

"And it was worth the risk," Sylvan muttered, looking down at the package in his hand, the package he had risked a bifurcation to retrieve from the two dead men.

And at that moment I remembered to wonder, for the first time, exactly what was in the package.

9

"*You* open it, Max," Sylvan said, back in the mobile home in 33,019 B.C. He tossed me the package he had collected from 1910 Bangkok.

I barely managed to catch it. It was wrapped in newspaper printed with Asian characters, tied with white string. I looked across at him, suddenly unsure. He smiled at me.

"Go on, open it, Max," Eve said eagerly, sitting beside me on the white canvas couch.

It felt absurdly as though they were giving me a birthday present. I slit the string with my knife and carefully unwrapped the newspaper, which was very neatly folded into triangular shapes.

Inside it was a phaser.

"Huh?" It was so unexpected, so shocking, that I fumbled and almost dropped it. Instinctively, I wrapped my hands tightly around it. I couldn't think of anything to say.

"Well?" Sylvan's grin had become complacent; his teeth weren't that great, I noticed. "Aren't you going to insist on an explanation, like you always do?"

"I would, if I thought you could come up with one I'd believe." I was still angry—and scared—about the way he had interfered with the past.

"Sure I can." He radiated self-satisfaction. "I told you we've been tying up loose ends, tracing the debris. This phaser could have caused a lot of trouble. Now it won't."

"But wouldn't it have been destroyed by lightning if you'd just left the past alone? Or else it would have fallen into the water. Wasn't it *more* dangerous to intervene? How could it cause a lot of trouble at the bottom of that river?"

"Someone would have found it eventually, far, far in the future," Eve said seriously, staring at it in my hands. "Phasers have a way of being found. And then there would have been bifurcations, and chaos."

"But because you took it, won't there be a bifurcation because nobody *will* find it, then?"

"Maybe," Eve said. "But it will be a *safe* bifurcation. The timeline where the phaser is found will lead to chaos.

But now there will be a timeline *without* the phaser, which will continue on normally, without chaos. Isn't that worth the risk?"

"I . . . I guess so," I said, trying to picture it, wondering if she was really making sense.

"That's our long-range goal, Max: to try to preserve a timeline without chaos, unaffected by the phaser." Sylvan sighed, and I noticed that he seemed tired now, for the first time since I'd met him. "Building this thing was more of a burden than I ever imagined." He lit a cigarette. "The responsibility is enormous. Sometimes I wonder if it was worth all the cleaning up we're doing now."

"Oh, come off it," I said, disgusted by his holier-than-thou attitude. "You made chaos yourself by swindling all that money from the stock market. If you hadn't done that, you wouldn't *have* all this cleaning up to do."

"You're right, Max," he said, looking at me directly, not smiling now. "We're rich, but we'll probably spend the rest of our lives paying for it, picking up the pieces."

He sounded sincere, but I still didn't believe him. What was a phaser doing in 1910 Bangkok in the first place? How had he traced it to that exact moment? I was about to ask him to explain, but then thought of something else. "So what are you going to do with this phaser now? If it has a way of being found, why is it any safer here than at the bottom of that river?"

"Because it's not going to stay here. I'm getting rid of it, destroying it."

"How?" I demanded skeptically. "And how can you ever prove to me that you really *are* destroying it?"

"Simple." Leaving the cigarette burning in the ashtray, he came over and sat down on the couch, on the other side of me from Eve. "Watch me, Max." He held out his hand for me to give him the phaser.

I didn't want to. Crazy as it was, I would have fought him to keep it, if it hadn't been for the other one in my protopack. But it was still with a feeling of great reluctance that I handed it over.

He took his own phaser from his pack and touched the one from Bangkok to the rough surface. It registered as specimen 527.23. I watched him type in the commands to send it 4.5 billion years into the past. I turned and looked at him questioningly.

"The molten earth, Max. I love thinking about it. This phaser will never show up again." He set the Bangkok phaser on the table and pressed ACTIVATE. It vanished.

All three of us watched the empty space on the table for a moment. I tried to imagine the inferno where he had just sent this thing we risked so much to find. I thought about the fact that I was registered on his phaser. At any moment he could send me to the molten earth. And he wanted me to put the others in the same defenseless position.

He got up and strolled toward the kitchen, turning in the doorway. "Anybody else want a beer?" he asked. Eve and I shook our heads.

As soon as he was out of the room she whispered, "I understand you, Max; I know why you're upset. You don't play games, you're genuine." She touched my arm with perfectly manicured fingernails. "I'm like that too."

"Then why didn't you warn me what was going to happen—that we were going into the past to steal that phaser? It was just the same as lying to me."

She sighed, but didn't look away. I noticed that her eye makeup was slightly smudged. Was it from tears, or just the Bangkok rain? "That's the way Dad wanted it," she said, more softly. "I never actually lied to you. But he was sure you'd make trouble if we told you."

We could hear Sylvan whistling as he poked through the refrigerator. I shook my head slowly. "So you always just go along with what he wants? Even if it's dangerous, or criminal?"

"Dad made mistakes, but I'm pretty sure he wants to fix them now. It might not seem that way, I know he has a crazy streak. Sometimes . . . I'm kind of afraid of him." She looked down into her lap, then back to me. "That's why I need you," she said quickly, to get the words out before Sylvan returned. "You're so blatantly honest. You might bring out something *good* in him. Please help me, Max."

She stopped talking at the sound of the refrigerator door being shut. I hadn't realized until now that there was a vulnerable side to her nature. It made me feel closer to her, a little protective. She really did seem to understand how I felt, and to need my help.

Sylvan came back and sat across from us again and took a long swig from a bottle of beer, watching me alertly. "Well, Max?" he said, swallowing. "Any more thoughts about that little favor I want you to do for me?"

"So you can send *them* 4.5 billion years into the past?" I

blurted out. "*Not* just to get rid of them because they know about you, and they might interfere with your fun. Oh, no, you're bigger than that. You just want to get rid of them because it's the only way to preserve one timeline without chaos. Is that what you're trying to make me believe?"

"As a matter of fact, yes," he said with a crooked smile, his elbows on his knees, holding the bottle of beer in both hands.

I snorted.

He snorted back at me. "Listen, kid, you're *lucky* I'm giving you the chance to prove yourself this way." His voice was not charming at all. "I could always just send you where I sent that phaser from Bangkok and deal with the others myself." He smiled at me in a way that made the back of my neck twitch. "Of course it *would* be easier for you to catch them unawares. So—I'm offering you a chance to save yourself. I think it's pretty damned generous, given the risk *I'm* taking by letting you get anywhere near the others with a phaser on you."

Eve smiled quickly at me, then glared at Sylvan. "Dad, you're *disgusting!* Don't talk nonsense. Max might think you mean it."

"Nonsense?" I asked her, cold all over, my voice catching in my throat. "You already told me he'd really do it. And now you expect me to believe he's kidding?"

"Yeah, Max, just kidding," Sylvan said, all geniality again, lifting his beer to me. "Except for the part about the risk I'm taking, giving you the chance to do this. You have to understand what's at stake here. I know you don't

84

want to *force* me to send you to the molten earth. But if you let them get that phaser . . ." He didn't need to finish the sentence.

Eve took my hand. "Please, Max, believe me, we don't want to hurt them. But as long as they're around, there's always the chance they could get the phaser, and send everything into chaos. They could get rid of *us*. Is *that* what you want to happen?"

"Well, no, but . . ."

"You don't sound too sure about it!" she snapped, sitting up straighter, her eyes flashing.

"But . . . It's just that . . ."

"Max!" Now she sounded hurt. "I thought you *liked* me."

I sighed, feeling manipulated and also embarrassed. "I *do* like you," I admitted. It was an understatement—I more than liked her—though it wasn't easy for me to say it. I had never felt this way about any girl before. "But . . ." I shook my head. "Why does that mean I have to help you two *kill* those people?"

"Who said anything about *killing* them?" she asked. "Dad just wants to fix it so they won't kill *us*—and believe me, they would, as soon as they got the chance."

"But why do you want them registered on the phaser if he's *not* going to send them back 4.5 billion years?"

"Think, Max. Yes, that was the only way to get rid of that phaser, because you can't send a phaser into the future—that would be a sure bifurcation. But *they're* not a phaser. Sending them to the future won't make a bifurcation, it won't kill them—and it will save us. That's all we want to do." She squeezed my hands, hard, then took her hands away and pressed her lips together and stared at me.

"You just want to send them to the future?" I asked Sylvan.

He nodded.

I tried to think rationally, scientifically, but it wasn't easy with Eve's gray eyes on me. What she had said *seemed* to make sense.

"You saw how careful I was, Max," Sylvan reminded me. "You saw all the work I've been doing to try to make this timeline safe again. All I'm asking is for you to help me with that."

"And to protect us, Max," Eve murmured, not taking her eyes away from me.

"After all, Max," Sylvan said lightly, "You can't expect me to let you keep your own phaser unless you prove I can trust you with it."

If I didn't do this, I'd have to relinquish it. The thought of that gave me a strange, empty feeling. And I knew Sylvan meant what he said: Helping him was the only way I could keep the phaser and use it.

I cleared my throat. "Well," I began, "Let's say I did register them on my phaser—not that I'm promising anything—but if I did . . . then could *I* be the one to set the controls? Just to be sure they *weren't* going 4.5 billion years into the past? If I could do it myself, so I'd be sure they wouldn't get hurt, then maybe I'd think about it."

"Why do you care so much about *them?*" Eve said.

"It's not a question of caring. I won't let them get killed.

Period. You said you didn't have to kill them. I just want to have some control so I can be sure."

Eve turned away from me to look at her father. After a moment, he nodded. "I don't see why not," he said, and drained the bottle. "As long as we all decide where we send them, and agree it's safe, why shouldn't Max push the buttons?"

"And you'd really let me keep my phaser? And take my number off yours?" I asked him.

"I told you I would."

Eve turned back to me, beginning to smile. "So you'll do it?"

"I said I'd *think* about it."

"Oh, *Max!*" she cried, and threw her arms around me. "You're *wonderful!* I *knew* I could count on you, I just *knew* it!"

My arms slipped around her as though drawn by a magnet. I pulled her closer.

"Come and get me when you're ready," Sylvan said, getting up to leave the room. "We'll take Max home, back to where he left his car, as soon as he wants."

"I hope it won't be *too* soon, though," Eve whispered.

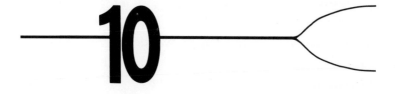

We left about an hour later, Eve and Sylvan in the front seat of the jeep, and headed for the spot in 33,019 B.C. where my house would be in the twentieth century. They quizzed me for details about the other Eve and Sylvan's appearance, and I told them, seeing no reason not to.

"When are they going to pick up the jacket from the cleaners?" Sylvan wanted to know.

"Thursday."

"Day after tomorrow. You have plenty of time." He glanced at me in the rearview mirror for a moment, then back outside. "I just hope you can carry it off."

"Max will do fine. But what a bore to have to grow my hair long, to look like *her*," Eve complained, sighing as she leaned forward in the front seat, peering out the windshield.

"Hey, that's not as bad as growing a pot belly," Sylvan said.

It was dark inside the bumping jeep. For the moment, they were not thinking about me. Very carefully, I un-zipped the phaser from my protopack and turned it on. Keeping my hand low, where they couldn't see it from the front seat, I registered the Jeep Cherokee as specimen 17.1, not knowing quite why. I got the phaser back inside just before Sylvan glanced at me again in the rearview mirror.

"The main thing, Max, is *not* to let them get the phaser. Do *anything* to prevent it. But I don't need to tell you that, do I? You know where you'll end up if anything goes wrong." He lifted his phaser, caught my eye in the mirror, and smiled.

I looked away, thinking of the molten earth.

"Oh, Dad, stop it," Eve said. "You know we can trust him."

"Sure, sure," he said. "It shouldn't be difficult, Max. Until Thursday, they won't suspect you have a phaser. That's what makes you so pivotal: You have a phaser and they don't know it. That's the real beauty of it."

He didn't let me take a hoverpack. He and Eve wore them, and hoisted me up by the armpits to a precise spot somewhere above the prairie in 33,019 B.C. Sylvan checked the same device on his wrist he had used to position us safely above the skyscraper in 2049, touching it to my feet, then telling me to lift them a few inches. "See you soon, Max," Eve said, and kissed me as Sylvan pressed the key.

The afternoon sun blinked on, and I fell to the ground a yard away from the stone wall at the entrance to our street. That was when the panic reaction hit. Only a slight miscalculation of Sylvan's would have landed me *inside* the wall. It brought home to me just exactly how impossible it would be to use my phaser to run away from him. I walked back to the car and slowly drove it home.

Mom and Dad were having drinks before dinner in the backyard, their same old plastic lawn chairs in the usual places. It was reassuring to know that they hadn't instantly become teetotalers, or suddenly acquired new lawn chairs. I was morbidly nervous about seeing any alterations in *my* timeline—that would mean our interference with the past had made a bifurcation.

"So, Max, did they have your calculator at the cleaners?" Mom asked.

"Yeah, they had the calculator," I said, sinking into a lawn chair. "I was really lucky."

"And then you went back to Eve's? Is that where you've been all day?"

I nodded. "They have a really fantastic house, with a waterfall and a pool and everything."

"He must be a real big shot at the labs," Dad said.

"I guess so."

Mom smiled. "Are you going to see her again?"

"Tomorrow," I said quickly. "Can I have the car? It's really important."

"Tomorrow?" Mom said. "Sure, I guess we can work it out."

"Thanks." I yawned. As Sylvan had predicted, I felt exactly as though I had jet lag. It made sense; it was only 6 P.M. here, but my watch said it was 5:30 A.M.

"So what did you find out about yesterday?" Mom asked me.

"Yesterday? Oh, that's right." So much had been going on that I had forgotten Mom and Dad would be curious about what supposedly had happened to me at the labs. "Um, it was . . . some kind of gas, part of an experiment Sylvan was doing. Just kind of knocked me out. But I'm fine now."

"You'd better go to bed early. You look pale," Mom said. "Oh, while I'm thinking about it, let me have the receipt, so I can get your jacket on Thursday."

"The receipt?" I thought of the Eve and Sylvan who had the receipt, and made a conscious effort not to squirm in the lawn chair. "Gee, I wonder where I put it. Just let me pick the jacket up myself. It'll be simpler."

"You didn't lose the receipt, did you? After all that fuss you made about it! I hope they won't give us any trouble claiming the jacket without it."

"No, no, they'll remember me. They don't find a phase . . . I mean a calculator in a jacket pocket every day."

At least I was hungry enough not to arouse any suspicions at dinner—the meal we had in 33,019 B.C. had been more than eight hours ago. I was glad to see Dad's preference in food hadn't changed; it was meat and potatoes, as usual. I tasted it carefully, checking for any unusual seasonings. But the food was as blandly familiar as ever. And after supper they both fell asleep in front of the TV. So far, so good. Maybe we hadn't made a bifurcation.

But upstairs in my room I began to worry again. Tired as I was, it still took me a while to get to sleep, lying in the darkness and worrying about what I had to do the next day, Wednesday, June 26. I had only one day before Sylvan would go to claim the jacket at the cleaners on Thursday. After that, it would be too late. Was I really going to carry it out? What would happen to the Eve who had kissed me if I didn't?

I already knew what would happen to me.

But I still didn't see how I could actually do this terrible thing to them. If only there were some other way! I tried to come up with an alternative, going over everything I knew about the phaser. Eventually I fell asleep. On Wednesday morning I was still no closer to a solution.

After Mom and Dad left for work, I paced, lifting the phone, then putting it down and walking away, then lifting and putting it down again. Fifteen minutes went by, a half hour. Finally I picked up the receiver and dialed.

An hour later I was ringing their apartment bell. Eve, in loose-fitting jeans and T-shirt, pulled me quickly inside. "Are you okay, Max? They didn't hurt you?" she immediately asked me, her face solemn with apprehension.

"I'm fine," I assured her. It was amazing how much she looked like the other Eve, but was still so different—so plain and nondescript.

Sylvan was in the kitchen. He studied me quickly. "You look a little ragged, Max," he said. "They weren't rough with you, I hope."

"No. Don't worry about me." I sat down slowly, glancing around the room. Sylvan didn't seem to have touched his breakfast of granola and yogurt and unbuttered whole wheat toast.

"You should really eat something, Dad," Eve gently urged him. "I could make you some oat bran."

These two seemed to eat nothing but health food, yet they looked so much less healthy than the others, who indulged in so many vices.

"Thank you, Eve. I'm not hungry," Sylvan said. "What happened, Max?"

"Like I told Eve on the phone, they were waiting for me near my house."

"Did they know you'd been here?"

"They assumed it. They . . . they knew you'd been trying to find me. It didn't seem logical to try to pretend anything else. They . . . they would have known I was lying about that."

Eve peered at me. "What's the matter with you today? You seem so jumpy."

"I *am* jumpy; I'm scared," I admitted. It was the truth. I didn't know what I was going to do.

Now that I was here with them, it seemed unthinkable that I could actually register them. I had a painful awareness that they were basically decent people. They weren't making an effort to win me over, like the others had. They seemed forthright and direct, not hiding from me how worried they were—not just about themselves, but about me as well. Even if the other Sylvan had no intention of sending them to the molten earth, it would still be a terrible punishment to condemn them to permanent exile in the future. What had they done to deserve that?

But what would these two do to the other Eve and Sylvan if I didn't do something to stop them? Now that I knew how I felt about her, I couldn't bear the thought of anything happening to the other Eve. And I had no doubt that her father *would* send me to the molten earth if I didn't get these two registered in time.

And yet, despite all of his excuses about preserving a stable timeline, I was still extremely reluctant to do anything that would help the other Sylvan—because of his blatant use of the phaser. No matter what he claimed, once the obstacle of these two was out of the way, he might very possibly drag this timeline into chaos, too, by making an accidental bifurcation.

I didn't know what to think. And I was going to have to do something soon, make a decision. Everything was riding on it. But I had no basis for a decision.

Unless I could find out a little more hard data about bifurcations from *this* Sylvan . . .

"What . . . what did you tell them?" Sylvan said apprehensively, as though he were afraid to know. Without waiting for an answer he turned to Eve. "We should have thought up a story for him, given him more help. Why didn't we do that? It wasn't fair to him. Now he's probably . . ." His voice faded.

"What matters is whether he told them about the jacket, and the dry cleaners, and the receipt," she said, in her straightforward, practical way. "You . . . you didn't tell them about that, did you?" she asked me.

I shook my head. It wasn't a complete lie. The others

hadn't been interested in all the details of how this Sylvan tried to hide the phaser, only in the fact of who had it now. But I still wanted to change the subject. If I played for time, maybe I could learn more from this Sylvan. "I acted dumb, like I still didn't know anything. It wasn't hard, since you two told me so little. I guess it *was* smart of you not to tell me much."

"And we can't tell you where the receipt is now," Eve said. "It's much safer that way. Did they believe you when you said you didn't know anything?"

Now what was I going to say? I didn't want to get into telling them out-and-out lies. I hated doing that, I was no good at it, and this Eve would probably catch me at it right away. But how much of the truth *could* I tell them?

And suddenly I wanted very much to tell them the truth, or at least part of it. This Sylvan was a lot more cautious and responsible than the other one. What would *he* think of the other Sylvan's claim that you could go into the past without making bifurcations as long as you were careful enough? If I knew that, I might have some basis for making a decision.

"Go on, Max," Eve prodded me. "Did they believe that you didn't know anything?"

"I . . . It's hard to be sure." I paused, wondering if this was the right thing to do, then plunged ahead. "Because right after that, they stopped asking me questions and . . . and took me into the past."

"*What?*" Sylvan rose to his feet, his face reddening. Eve stared hard at me, without expression. "Where into the past?" she said.

I wanted to tell them as much as I could, without making the other Eve vulnerable to them. "To . . . to 43,000 B.C.," I said, thinking quickly enough to give them the wrong date so they wouldn't be able to find the hideout if they ever did get a phaser. "They have a hideout there."

Sylvan sank back into his chair, his eyes riveted on me, his hands clenching into fists. "They actually go into the *past?*"

I nodded.

He turned to Eve, then quickly back to me. "But that's . . . that's monstrous, appalling! How *dare* they?"

For a moment I thought he was only horrified. Then he leaned forward, his breath coming quickly. "The past! What did it feel like, to travel that far on the phaser?" He was curious, even envious. He desperately wanted to know. The phaser had a hold on him, too. But I wouldn't let him take it from me!

"Tell me, Max!" he demanded. "What was it like there? What did you see? What did they—"

Eve's firm voice cut through his excited questions. "Why would they take you into the past if they *didn't* think you knew anything about the phaser?"

She was sharp all right; her question made a lot of sense. And how could I answer her, without giving away the fact that I had the phaser and the others knew it? "The other Sylvan couldn't resist, he likes showing off," I said lamely. "And maybe they just wanted to share it with me because they like me—that's what they said, anyway." I turned quickly to Sylvan, not just to change the subject, but also because I really couldn't hold back my questions any longer. "The other Sylvan claims he can construct bifurcation-free windows in the past. He says bifurcations don't happen unless you change something on a human scale. Is that true? Couldn't just breathing *air* in the past lead to a bifurcation? Where do you draw the line?"

Sylvan's eyes were wide and alert now. "That's exactly the question I've been working on, Max. These last two days, while we've been cooped up here. How large or small a change is necessary to make a bifurcation? How long it takes the displacement of two molecules to lead to a human change, if ever. Strange attractors, and the sensitive dependence on initial conditions. And I think I'm getting some answers."

"Go on," I urged him. "What answers?"

"It's fascinating, Max! The other Sylvan might possibly be right about some things, after all. Just going into the past doesn't automatically make a bifurcation. The equations show that. If you were extraordinarily careful, you might be able to get away with it, *without* bringing on chaos. Did you know that—"

"Dad," Eve cautioned him, touching his arm.

"But, Eve . . ." He turned toward her, startled.

"Please! I've *got* to know!" I blurted out.

"I know you need to talk about it, Dad, I know Max honestly wants to understand." She smiled briefly at me, not the playful, teasing smile of the other Eve, not an expression that lit up her face, but merely a sober affirmation that she understood my curiosity. "But don't you both see how dangerous it is for Max to know anything? If he ever sees them again, the more *he* knows, the more he'll be able to tell them—even if he doesn't want to. And the more *they* know, the more they can use against us. The only way we'll ever get through this is to be extremely careful."

For a moment I was angry. There was so much I needed to know! But quickly I saw that Eve was right. From their point of view, there was nothing to gain—and everything to lose—from telling me anything at all. I couldn't blame her for being careful. I had to respect her for being so wise. It cheered me a little to know, in my dilemma, that her survival instincts were so highly developed.

And I was even more cheered by the information Sylvan had just given me. It seemed to indicate that the other Sylvan was not as irresponsible as I had thought, that the timeline was not so vulnerable after all. Maybe I had learned enough; I began to see the beginnings of a plan, a solution. But I needed a chance to think about it, alone. "I guess it *is* better, for everybody, if I don't know too much," I said, standing up. "Now, uh, how do I get to the bathroom?"

Sylvan told me, but I went past the bathroom and quickly checked out the bedrooms first, so I wouldn't have trouble finding them, if I really did decide to carry this thing through. Across from the bathroom was Sylvan's study, a small, windowless room. A computer glowed on the desk, which was littered with papers. Books and magazines were stacked on the floor in two precarious piles. Next came Sylvan's bedroom, with more scientific journals on a table beside the bed. Eve's room was down the hall, with a small desk and a single bed. Everything was very neat, the bed carefully made. But I was surprised to see a whole collection of stuffed furry animals on the shelves, bed, and floor. They seemed out of character for such a competent and down-to-earth person.

Inside the bathroom, I turned on the light and tested the door, as I had tested all the others. Fortunately, the only one that squeaked was Sylvan's study, which wouldn't matter. I clicked the lock on the bathroom door.

It was a small room, with red and blue wallpaper in a large flowered pattern that made me feel slightly claustrophobic. I closed my eyes and tried to think clearly.

And the plan took shape more solidly in my mind. The more I thought about it, the more sure I became that I *could* register them without their knowing about it. The question was: Should I do it?

I was no longer so worried about how they would do in the future. It would be a shock at first, but I was pretty sure now, seeing Eve's calm and rational behavior under stress, that she would be able to adapt to it. As for Sylvan, he would probably be thrilled to be able to witness firsthand the advances in science and technology.

And the other Eve needed my help.

I also knew that if I backed down, and decided not to register them, Sylvan would no doubt find some other way to send them into the future. It would be more difficult, but he was wily and determined enough to do it. By not registering them myself, I wouldn't be saving them.

I would only be condemning *myself* to the molten earth. They'd still end up in the future—and I would be dead.

It seemed very clear to me now that I really had no choice. There was only one reasonable course of action— to register them now. I took the phaser out of my proto-pack, aware of the anticipatory thrill that seemed to go along with using it.

Then I remembered that the bathroom lock had made an audible click, so I unlocked the door, leaving it open a quarter of an inch. I got out my pocket flashlight and tested it. That reminded me to turn off the bathroom light. I sat down on the closed toilet seat in the semidarkness. I went over the plan again, step by step, concentrating on all the details. I took off my shoes.

I switched on the phaser. I had a sense of its power flowing up my arm, rising through my body, as the numbers blossomed across the display. It was now 11:23 A.M., June 26. I set the controls to send myself sixteen hours into the future. I turned on the faucet in the sink, to cover the sound of the beep. I lifted my finger to press ACTIVATE.

But I hesitated, worrying. Was I forgetting something?

I reminded myself that if I didn't do this, I wouldn't be saving *this* Eve and Sylvan, I would only be sending my-self to the molten earth. And the other Eve would have to find someone else to help her.

I pressed ACTIVATE.

The bathroom light blinked on, the door sprang open, my shoes vanished. I panicked, knowing I had left the light off, the door closed, and the shoes beside the toilet. I checked the time on the phaser. It was 3:23 A.M., June 27.

I tried to calm myself. Naturally my shoes weren't here now. I would have taken them with me when I left the bathroom at 11:25 yesterday morning. And of course they had used the bathroom since then, leaving the door open and the light on. I was going to have to be very, very careful. Still, the disappearance of my shoes did give me hope that I would get this done and return safely.

I remained motionless and listened. I reminded myself that I didn't have to hurry, I could take all the time I needed. What mattered most was not waking them up. I sat quietly. But I couldn't hear anything in the rest of the apartment because the bathroom fan was humming; it was obviously controlled by the light switch. I cursed whoever had been careless enough to leave it on.

I carefully set the phaser for the return trip—in case I had to get back fast—and finally forced myself to stand. From inside the bathroom, against the wall, I peeked out into the hallway. It really was bad luck that the bathroom light was on, because all I could see was the bright parallelogram it cast on the hallway floor. Everything else was pitch-dark in contrast, and my eyes wouldn't adjust until I took the risk of stepping out of here. I could only hope they really were both in bed, and asleep.

I moved out of the bathroom. Keeping my back against the wall, where floorboards were less likely to creak, I inched down the hallway toward the bedrooms. As soon as I was several feet away from the patch of light from the bathroom I stopped and stared fixedly into the darkest corner, waiting for my eyes to adjust. There had to be a little light from outside, maybe enough to see by, and I didn't want to use the flashlight unless it was absolutely necessary.

Eve, more alert and quick-thinking than Sylvan, would be the real danger, so I had decided to deal with her first, get it over with. There was a little gray light from the window at the end of the hallway and I was beginning to be able to distinguish the vague shapes of things. As I approached Eve's room I saw that the door was slightly ajar. At least I would not have to fumble with the door-knob. I stopped, standing against the wall opposite her door. I took a deep breath and stepped toward it. A floor-board creaked, very faintly, and I froze. After fifteen seconds of silence I stepped forward again. Holding my breath, I pushed open Eve's door, very slowly, and entered her room.

There were no shades behind the filmy transparent curtains, and I had no trouble seeing her shape on the bed. My heart was pounding so violently that it seemed to fill the room, but I told myself there was no way she could possibly hear it. I forced myself to move, remembering to watch for any stuffed animals on the floor; the carpet kept my footsteps silent. I was a nervous wreck, but so far nothing had gone wrong. Maybe I would actually carry this off.

I stood just beside the bed, the phaser outstretched in my hand. Eve slept on her side, her back to the room, her unbraided hair spread out on the pillow. Her left arm curled around a worn old bear, her pale face pressed against its patchy dark fur. And suddenly I saw her as a defenseless little girl, clinging to the toy for comfort and protection. What would her life be like in that alien future world? Could I really do this?

She shifted, and mumbled something. I pulled my hand back, my heart going crazy.

But I couldn't just stand here, I had to act. I reached out with the phaser, holding it an inch away from her face. And then I had an idea. It was just a little thing, but it might just possibly give her a tiny bit of comfort, later. Very carefully, I brushed the textured surface of the phaser against her fingernail where it pressed into the bear's fur, making sure to touch the bear at the same time, registering them both together as specimen 18.1.

She shifted again, but her eyes did not open. I turned away, unable to look at her a moment longer, and crept out into the hallway. I faltered, leaning against the wall, suddenly weak. It was just as though I had stabbed her in her sleep.

But I couldn't stop now, in the middle. I told myself I *hadn't* sentenced her to a miserable existence somewhere in the future. She wasn't under the other Sylvan's control yet. That wouldn't happen until Sylvan got his hands on this phaser. And maybe he never would.

But I was horribly edgy now; I wanted to get this over with as soon as possible. I entered Sylvan's bedroom, where there was also enough light to see without the flashlight. I approached the bed more quickly, a little less cautious now.

And then my heart seemed to stop. His bed was empty.

I squeezed my eyes shut, clenching my fists. *Where was he?* If he were out of the apartment, I'd have to go through this whole thing all over again, another time, which was unthinkable. But that wasn't very likely. He could be awake, in the kitchen, having a snack. He could be in his study, working on his equations. In either case, I was done for. My impulse was to head for the bathroom and get out of here fast.

But I waited, and listened carefully in the hallway.

There were no noises from the study, or from the kitchen. And the most likely possibility occurred to me: He might have fallen asleep at his desk.

His study door was firmly closed. Gritting my teeth, but desperate enough now to risk it, I twisted the knob and pushed the door. It made a noise, I froze, then pushed it far enough to get through. Inside, it was too dark to see a thing. The room was windowless, I remembered, and the light from the bathroom fell in the other direction, giving me no help at all. I thought of the piles of books and magazines on the floor. I told myself he probably wasn't in here after all—if he had fallen asleep at his desk, the light or the computer would still have been on.

Unless Eve, ever solicitous of her father, had turned them off before going to bed herself. I had to make sure. I switched on the flashlight.

The narrow beam landed directly on his face. He was slumped forward in the desk chair, his head on a pile of papers beside the computer keyboard, facing the door. He grunted, and rolled his head. I instantly turned off the flashlight, sweat breaking out over my entire body.

I listened to the rustle of his head on papers, to his wet gulping noises. They gradually subsided. But he seemed to be a light sleeper. Which would be more likely to wake him? The flashlight beam guiding me on the floor, or the crash of me knocking down a pile of books, the inevitable alternative? I decided the flashlight would be safer; books falling might wake Eve as well.

The tension was really getting to me now, ringing in my ears, every nerve in my body jumpy and haywire. I felt as though I'd just been in a car accident. Another minute would be too much of this. I switched on the flashlight, my eyes on the floor, taking little steps around the books. Finally I reached the desk. I held out the phaser and looked down at Sylvan in the light reflected from the beam on the floor.

"Huh?" He mumbled, blinking.

I touched the phaser to his back, registering him as specimen 19.1, then turned and ran from the room, knocking books all over the place. I pulled the bathroom door shut and clicked the lock, not worrying about the consequences. I had set the phaser so that three seconds after pressing ACTIVATE it would bring me back to 11:25 yesterday morning. I checked it again, hoping I'd left myself a safe margin of error. I pressed ACTIVATE.

In the three remaining seconds I took one more fast precaution. I jumped up from the toilet and sat down on the edge of the tub, just in case I had blundered and would arrive before I left.

The doorknob turned. "Wait!" Sylvan shouted. "Unlock the—"

His voice stopped abruptly. The light went off, the door jumped open a quarter of an inch, water burst from the sink faucet, and my shoes appeared beside the empty toilet seat.

I'd done it! I was safely back in the present, and they were registered on the phaser.

Except that Sylvan was going to be awakened by me at 3:30 tomorrow morning. What messy effect on events would that have? Had I broken my promise to keep my possession of the phaser a secret from them? I wasn't sure. They didn't know it yet. I started to put on my shoes, my heart still beating wildly, trying to figure it out.

And then I saw what I had forgotten.

12

They weren't talking as I entered the kitchen. Walking past them in the uncomfortable silence, I was acutely aware of the weight of the phaser in my protopack. I told myself there was no way they could see the shape of it through the leather. But I was glad that it was hidden by the table when I sat down.

"What's the matter?" Eve asked me.

"Huh?" I clenched my hands together in my lap. What else had I overlooked, what other horrible mistake had I made? "The matter? What do you mean?"

"You look sick." I couldn't tell from her voice whether

she was suspicious, or merely concerned about me. "Your face is actually *green*."

"Oh. Yeah, I guess I do feel kind of sick," I said truthfully. "This whole thing is a little much to take. I'm scared, like I said before."

"He must be somewhat out of sync, too, because they took him into the past," Sylvan reminded her. Then another thought struck him and he turned to me, putting his hand to his mouth. "That must mean . . . you're registered on his phaser."

I nodded at him, swallowing.

"And at any moment, the other Sylvan could . . ." He stared at me, his shoulders sagging. "It's my fault, Eve," he said numbly. "Max was innocent, and he's trapped now. The other Sylvan could kill him in an instant; he could do things *worse* than killing him. And it's just the same as if I did it to him myself."

She opened her mouth to speak, most likely to point out some reason why Sylvan shouldn't blame himself. But the words didn't come. She watched me, some sort of inward struggle going on behind her guarded expression. Then she turned to her father. "But isn't there *anything* we can do to protect Max? To make him safe again?" The unexpected urgency in her voice startled me.

"Not without getting our hands on the other Sylvan's phaser. That would solve everything, of course. But you know that's . . ." He shook his head miserably. "About all we can do is register Max on my phaser, if we manage to get it tomorrow. That won't be much protection for him, though."

Eve turned back to me. "Max, I guess . . ." She sighed,

uncomfortable about what she was going to say, but determined to go on. "Well, you *did* make it easy for them, Max. You told them too much the first time. And I still have no proof that we can really trust you. But . . . if we can get you out of this, we'll do it. We'll do anything we can. You made some mistakes, so did we. But we didn't mean for this to happen to you."

My throat tightened. I couldn't look at her, I couldn't think of any words, I wanted to disappear. I shrank into the chair, squeezing my hands between my knees. Two decent people. What had I done to them? "Oh, that's okay," I finally managed to say, my voice sounding like someone else's. "You didn't mean it. Maybe . . . things will work out."

She stared at me, obviously surprised at the way I sounded. "Well, I hope so," she said, businesslike again. "And you could help by telling us more about the others."

I tried to make my voice sound normal. "Well, you know, they look just like you. Except she has short hair and wears makeup. And he . . . he looks more like an athlete than a scientist."

She sighed with irritation. "I don't mean what they *look* like, Max. I mean what their plans are, what they've told you, what they want. You know more about them than anybody. If we're going to protect ourselves from them, all three of us, if we're ever going to be safe again, you're going to have to be completely open with us."

I tried to smile at her. Why hadn't I known it would be like this? Guilt of this magnitude was a new emotion,

110

changing everything, like a layer of grime over the world. It left me strangely exposed, as in a dream in which you are naked but no one else has noticed it yet. All I wanted was to get out of here as soon as possible. I'd accomplished what I'd set out to do. And getting away from them would have been an inexpressible relief.

The most crushing pain was the obvious fact I had somehow forgotten until it was too late: These two were the ones who belonged in this timeline; they were innocent. The others *were* impostors, scheming to get rid of them and take their places. And I had opened the way for them. Being here was torture. But I had to prolong it.

Because as soon as I left, Sylvan would find me. He would want to use the phaser, which had their specimen numbers on it now.

"Max, what *is* the matter with you?" Eve said. "You seem so different all of a sudden. Why won't you answer me?" She turned to her father. "He's hiding something; I *know* he is."

"If you want to know what they're really like," I said, "the scariest thing about them is the way they . . . I don't know, they kind of carry you away, make you forget things." That reminded me of something Sylvan had said yesterday. "You said the others were strange attractors. Does that mean that they have some kind of . . . unusual influence on people?"

Sylvan pushed back his unkempt hair. "That's what I've been suspecting. And as strange attractors, they are also a magnetic basin of instability in this timeline. They will pull us into chaos, by their very nature, their *wrong-*

ness. Unless we can get them out of this timeline before it's too late."

"What's too late?" I asked him. "How much time do we have left?"

"That's what I've been trying to find out. Some of the results are hopeful, some . . . worrisome." He pulled at his long hair. "You say they took you back to 43,000 B.C. Why that far?"

"Partly because it's empty, there aren't a lot of objects to bump into there—and a glacier's going to come and crush the remains of the hideout. But the most important reason is that the Siberians hadn't crossed over the land bridge from Asia yet. The continent is completely uninhabited by humans. He said that meant he couldn't make bifurcations there."

Sylvan nodded. "Possibly. Just breathing air in the past isn't too risky, not a particularly sensitive change. According to my calculations, there would have to be a change in initial conditions of—"

"Dad, *please!*" Eve interrupted him. Listening to him, I hadn't noticed how agitated she was becoming. "He could just go back and tell him! All your new research! At least let *him* tell *us* something first," she begged him. "You'd talk about science to anybody. Do you realize he hasn't even told us what the other Sylvan's plan is?"

"All right, Max," Sylvan said reluctantly. He'd been avoiding this too, burying his head in the less-threatening abstractions of science. "Tell us."

Looking at their anxious expressions, so strikingly different to me now from the deliberately self-confident faces of the others, I felt a sudden urge to tell them every-thing. Then I would have been partially clean again. And then the other Sylvan would kill me.

But that wasn't the only reason I couldn't tell them. If I did, they would take my phaser. And it was like part of my body now. Giving it up would be the same as cutting off a limb.

What was happening to me? Was it really me who had done this to them, and even now wouldn't confess it?

"Why did they let you come back here, anyway?" Eve wanted to know. "Was that part of their plan?"

I had to say something; otherwise I'd lose my phaser. "They think I'm on their side," I told her. "So, they wanted me to come back here to . . . to try to find out what you did with your phaser. They want to get rid of you. Not kill you. They would just . . . send you away so they can take your places here."

"Of course we know they want us registered," Eve said, peering at me curiously. "That's why we can't let them get our phaser. They'll never let anyone else carry the one they have. But if they had two, someone *else* could sneak in here and register us."

The way she was explaining it to me, so patiently, was the worst nightmare yet. I felt like screaming. If only I could wake up and find I hadn't done this to them! If only I could get out of here! But I was trapped in this room with all their questions.

"They must have been more specific, Max," Eve prodded me. "We can't trust you unless you tell us. *How* are they going to try to register us, with only one phaser? And what . . ." She hesitated. "Exactly what *would* they do to us, if we were registered?"

"*Not* 4.5 billion years ago, to the molten earth," I blurted out. "They promised. To the future. Somewhere in the future, where it wouldn't make a bifurcation. You wouldn't have a phaser, so you couldn't . . . couldn't get back here and try to do the same thing to them."

They looked at each other. "You sound like you really believed them," Eve said wonderingly.

"What do you mean?"

Sylvan smiled a little sadly at my naiveté. "I built the phaser, remember, Max. If the other Sylvan just sent me to the future, I could build it again, and come back to get him. There's no way he would take that risk. And there's no way he could send us alive into the past, somewhere where we could survive; that would make an immense bifurcation that would certainly affect him. No, Max, you've already said it: 4.5 billion years into the past, to the molten earth. That's the only thing he could do to us."

"He lied to me. And I believed him," I said, almost whispering. And I thought, the other Eve lied to me too. Had she been lying about everything? How much longer could I endure any of this?

"You didn't know who you were dealing with, Max," Eve said, in a tone of voice I'd only heard her use to her father before. She briefly touched my hand. "But you did the right thing, tricking them into thinking you were on their side. As long as you didn't tell them about the jacket, and the cleaners, then we still have a chance. But we'll have to give you a story to tell them about today." She looked away, twisting the end of her braid, thinking. The way her hair was pulled back made her face seem rounder than the other Eve's, her cheekbones less prominent. "*I* know. Tell them that we can't get our hands on the phaser until Saturday. Say you overheard it. That will put them off, make them think they have more time. Then maybe they won't interfere with . . . with how it's going to be picked up."

Their pathetic, botched little plan about the cleaners! Even *I* had seen through that, right away. These two were no match for the others. But they still had hope, they still thought they had a chance. In a way, they were heroes.

And as soon as I left . . .

"You better go now," Eve said briskly, shaking her shoulders to release some of her tension, the braid swinging across her back. "They must be watching from somewhere, they'll know how long you've been here. If you stay any longer they won't believe you learned so little, they'll be suspicious. And if they don't believe you, they may do something awful to you."

Her face was full of worry for me now. She touched my hand again, but this time she held onto it for a moment. "And . . . Thanks, Max. Thanks for helping us."

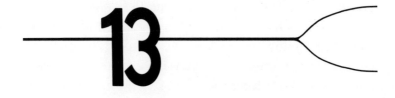

13

When and where would Sylvan come for me?

It seemed odd to me now, driving home, that he hadn't arranged a rendezvous, or even a way for me to contact them when my mission was completed. Was he waiting for me to telephone them at the house with the waterfall? I wouldn't, of course, even if I did get home.

Not that I was expecting to get home. Sylvan would find me before then. And then he would send the real Eve and Sylvan 4.5 billion years into the past.

And after that, what would stop Sylvan from doing the

same thing to me? All that protected me now was the phaser, with the real Eve and Sylvan's specimen numbers on it. Once he had that, I'd be done for. I saw now, too late again, that he couldn't let me stick around. I would know that he had ousted the real Eve and Sylvan from this timeline. I would be a threat to him, however minimal. He couldn't allow that threat to exist. And Eve wouldn't be able to stop him—even if she wanted to.

She hadn't been lying when she said there was a crazy side to him. I remembered the special way he had smiled whenever he mentioned sending me to the molten earth. He had actually *admitted* that he loved the thought of it. He wouldn't be sending me there only to protect himself; he would also be getting a kick out of it.

But even now, understanding all of this, I still seemed somehow to be under his control. Was this indefinable influence what had prevented me from giving the phaser to the real Eve and Sylvan? Or was it the addiction of the phaser—that I couldn't bear to be parted from it? Giving it up would have been the only way to try to save them, and to try to protect this timeline from chaos. Of course, doing that would have consigned me to the molten earth. But I would still be going to the molten earth anyway.

I continued to drive toward home. Could I still change things? Would Sylvan be able to catch me if I turned around and drove back to the apartment? I didn't know. I just kept driving. Was I doing this because they were strange attractors and I was under a kind of spell? Was it because I wanted to see Eve again, just for one last minute, even knowing that she had lied to me? Or did part of me still believe, against all logic and reason, that she hadn't lied, and Sylvan would let me live, let me keep the phaser, and not kill the others?

No. I knew that wasn't possible. And I knew that the only decent course of action would be to warn the others and give them the phaser. But I couldn't do it. For whatever reason, I had lost control. I couldn't even blame Sylvan for using the phaser to corrupt me. I had made all the wrong choices from the very beginning. In a strange way, it was almost a relief to know that, once I reached the molten earth, I wouldn't be able to do any more harm.

I turned onto our street. There was no Jeep Cherokee behind the wall. I parked in the driveway and went into the house, feeling very curious. Why weren't they waiting for me?

It was early afternoon. Mom and Dad were still at work. That was good; I didn't feel like talking to anybody. I went up to my room, more and more mystified. When was Sylvan going to strike? How was he going to get at me here?

Was it possible that something had gone wrong with *his* plans?

I laughed to myself, immediately dismissing that hope. He would get the phaser—though the thought of parting with it now was physically painful to me. Wondering how I would bear it, I lay down on the bed.

And then I fell. It was like that feeling of pitching forward that wakes you from half-sleep, except that it was real. They caught me under the arms, hovering like angels high above the prairie in 33,019 B.C.—as usual, Sylvan's timing was perfect. I managed not to scream, terrified, clinging instinctively to their shoulders with both arms. And almost before I knew it, while I was hanging there, helpless to fight him off, Sylvan had my protopack unzipped and my phaser in his own pouch. That was when I screamed.

They lowered me to the ground. The empty protopack felt like a hole cut out of my body.

Sylvan's hair was longer now; somehow, he had developed a pot belly. "Well, Max?" he said.

"Yeah, I did it."

He cried out, lifting both his arms. Now they were more jubilant than ever. Eve had managed to grow a shortish braid; I could never mistake her for the real one, but everyone else probably would. I hated her long hair and what it meant, but somehow I still couldn't hate her.

In the jeep, Sylvan told me they had been away in the future for three months, taking time to change their appearance. "We broke our rule for that, but never again. From now on we stay strictly in the same time frame."

"I thought about you the whole time we were away, Max," Eve whispered, sitting beside me in the back, wearing her slinky black jumpsuit. Even now, in my wretched state, the strange pleasure of being close to her diminished the pain of needing the phaser. But she had lied to me. I slid away, squeezing against the door, looking for something to distract me from her.

My eyes happened to fall on the elaborate dashboard. One of the instruments was a compass. We were traveling northeast, from the starting point of my house. The real

Eve and Sylvan's apartment building was also directly northeast of my house. I checked the odometer when the mobile home came into view. It also seemed to be just about the same distance. Sylvan had been telling me the truth when he said that the mobile home occupied the same space as the basement of Eve and Sylvan's apartment building in the twentieth century. With that location, it would be easy to keep tabs on the real Eve and Sylvan, and easy to get here from the apartment when they took it over. And how soon would they do that?

Inside the mobile home I sat down in the chair rather than the couch, so Eve couldn't sit beside me. "You figure out the specimen numbers," I told Sylvan. "Go ahead. Get it over with."

Sylvan, jauntily attired in white pants with dolphins on them, seemed genuinely puzzled, as well as amused. "I thought you wanted to push the buttons yourself, Max," he said, humoring me, as though my mood were childish. "I was expecting you to hold out for that."

"What is the *matter* with you, Max?" Eve demanded, looking hurt. "You haven't said one word to me."

"You lied," I said instantly. "Your father can't send the other Eve and Sylvan into the future. Sylvan would build another phaser and come back. He *has* to send them 4.5 billion years into the past and kill them. You lied to me because you knew I wouldn't do it if I knew."

Eve rolled her eyes. "Is *that* all it is?" she said with relief, and sank down onto the couch.

"Yes, that's all," I said. "You lied to me so I'd help him kill them, and I don't like it. Silly of me, isn't it?"

"That's what they told you, Max?" Sylvan asked me, his grin spreading. "That we would have to kill them because it wasn't safe sending them into the future? And you believed them, and registered them for me anyway?" He turned to Eve. "You were right all along," he congratulated her. "This kid really has potential."

It was the most terrible thing I had ever done in my life, and he loved me for it. "Just shut up and *do* it!" I shouted.

"Max, Max, pull yourself together," Sylvan said, patting the air comfortingly. "Eve didn't lie to you. I'm not going to kill them. You seem to forget that they don't know as much as we do, haven't seen what we've seen. They don't know that I *can* send them into the future and still be safe from them—as long as I make sure it's a *chaotic* future I send them to."

This was something I hadn't been expecting. "A chaotic future?" I murmured. "What exactly does *that* mean?"

"Oh. I guess I *did* forget to mention that part," Eve said. She leaned urgently toward me. "But it's true, Max. I wasn't lying, you have to believe me. They can't get out of chaos without a phaser, and they can't build one there, either—chaotic time is too peculiar. They'll be okay there, sort of. So now you can relax—since you still seem to care about *them* so much." She sat back and folded her arms, glaring at me.

Could I believe her? Was it possible that she really didn't know what Sylvan had to do to me? "Chaos?" I asked Sylvan. "Is that where you're going to send me, too?"

Sylvan had taken a phaser out of his yellow pack. It

wrenched me to look at it. He squatted down beside the coffee table, punching keys, then glanced up at me. "Sure, Max," he said lightly. "You wanted to see chaos. Now you will."

"What?" Eve's voice was suddenly so faint and cold that she sounded like another person. I turned back to her. Her face was deathly pale. "Dad?" she said, and licked her bright red lips. "You're kidding, of course."

She hadn't been lying to me. She did need me. She had really believed Sylvan would let me stay.

"Oh, Eve, get realistic." He was trying to sound casual about it, but he couldn't face her, a tic trembling in his left eye. He held himself stiff with tension, squatting there by the table. "Max understands. Sure, he has potential. But he *knows* too much. If we keep him around—"

Eve howled, a sound unlike anything I'd ever heard before, and rushed at him. She pushed him to the floor. He fended her off with his right hand, pressing ACTIVATE with the other.

With a phaser maybe I'd be able to get myself, and the others, out of chaos—whatever chaos was going to be like. I lunged out of the chair, grabbing wildly for his left hand, hungry for the phaser. Eve shoved her knee at his crotch. I wrapped my fingers around his wrist. My thumb touched the phaser; pleasure shot through me. In another second, with her help, maybe I *could* get

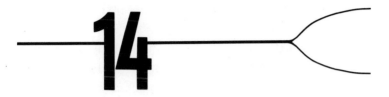

14

A feeble scream.

I hit the floor on my hands and knees, my brief fall cushioned by sheets and towels and underwear. In the unsteady light, it took me a moment to see the streaks of filth on the fabric. I scrambled to my feet, wiping my hands on my pants.

Machines lined the walls. There were no windows. The bright tubes on the ceiling flickered maddeningly, light dancing and ricocheting across their length as if the neon couldn't make up its mind where to go next.

A machine popped open above me and vomited out more laundry, wet and slimy with detergent. Darting out of its way, my feet tangled in a garment on the floor and I keeled over. I lay there, catching my breath.

I didn't get the phaser. I could still feel the spot where my thumb had touched it, aching with the loss of it. Without it I was stuck here, in some chaotic timeline.

I remembered the chaotic veil on the graph, the sick feeling of excitement it had given me. Now I would find out what chaos was like. I would spend the rest of my life finding out.

I tried to tell myself that I was incredibly lucky just to be alive. Sylvan hadn't bothered to position me in space this time, and by all reasonable odds I should have ended up inside some solid object and been blown to bits. But somehow I had landed safely in this basement laundry room of the future. There were complicated controls on the grimy transparent machines; the walls and floor were covered with some deeply textured, mosslike material; there was a lounge area with bulbous, comfortable-looking furniture and a wall-sized video screen. And yet, elaborate and futuristic as it all was, nothing seemed to be working very well.

"Chaos," I whispered, getting to my feet again. Was this all chaos was going to be—a life spent with drearily malfunctioning machines?

"Where'd you come from?" someone said.

I jumped, and turned around. An elderly woman was crawling out from underneath a table in the center of the room; she must have hidden there when she saw me fall out of nowhere. Short and plump, she wore a shapeless garment that seemed to change color in the shifting light. She pointed a little knife at me. "I said, where'd you come from, out of the air like that?" she asked me again, breathing heavily. "Don't come any closer!" She spat the words out so quickly I could barely understand them as she gestured shakily with the knife, terrified of me.

"I'm not going to hurt you," I said, lifting my hands to show I had no weapon.

"How'd you get here?"

What could I tell her? Did it really matter, in chaos? "It's hard to explain. I'm lost. I don't want anything from you. I just want to get home." There was a doorway at the far end of the room. I moved toward it slowly, keeping my hands in the air, staying on the other side of the table from her. "See? I'm just on my way out."

She kept the knife pointed at me, turning as I crossed the room. "I'm . . . I'm . . . reporting . . . this," she drawled, speaking so slowly now she sounded as though she were falling asleep. That, and the vagueness of the threat, suggested she wasn't sure who she would report it to.

"Please, just tell me one thing," I said, pausing in the doorway. I was pretty sure this was the right building, but I wanted to be certain about it. I gave her the real Eve and Sylvan's address, and asked her if that was where we were now.

"How'd you get here, if you don't know where it is?"

"Please, just tell me. What difference will it make? I'm already here. I just want to know if that's this building's address."

She nodded.

"Oh, and uh, what's the date?" I took the risk of asking her.

"Date? I don't know what you mean." The words tumbled out in a staccato barrage. "Now get out, before I— before I—"

"Thanks." I stepped out of the room. This was the right building, but were the real Eve and Sylvan here, too, in this exact moment, whenever it was? I was almost sure I had seen three specimen numbers on Sylvan's phaser in the last seconds before it beeped. I couldn't see any reason why he *shouldn't* have sent all of us to the same moment, since none of us had a phaser. And I wanted the real Eve and Sylvan to be here. I had to find them.

I started down the long hallway. The lights here were also flickering, the floor covered with the same mosslike material, damp and slightly squishy beneath my feet. There only seemed to be one other person in the corridor, far ahead of me, another stroke of luck. Eve and Sylvan would probably be having problems in the apartment. I began to run.

They would hate me, of course. They would probably never forgive me. Why should they? But knowing two people from home, even two people who hated me, would be better than being here alone. They ought to be glad to know I was in the same fix I'd put them in. It was even possible that we might be able to help each other somehow.

I passed a doorway. There were actually several people in the corridor; I just didn't seem to have noticed them at first. A man pushed past me, knocking me against a child.

I started to apologize, but the child was already swept away. This section of the corridor was jammed with people. I didn't understand where they had come from so unexpectedly. None of them had blinked into existence out of nowhere, like I had in the laundry room. They were all suddenly in the middle of busy errands. I must have been too distracted to notice them coming.

I worked my way through the slowly moving crowd, trying not to go crazy with impatience, looking for a stairway. I needed to get up to the ground floor, to the front lobby where I'd been before, so I would know how to find their apartment. The corridor turned left, there was a kind of lobby, with three elevators. "The stairs, where are the stairs?" I asked the people who were pressed immediately against me.

"If you have to ask, that means you don't live here," a woman barked rapidly at me.

"But I just want to—"

"You gotta have a key for the stairs," a man said. "Visitors take the elevators."

But how would I even get on an elevator? The crowd was tighter than ever here. And if the elevators were anything like the lights and the laundry machines, they would be malfunctioning, and very likely to be unsafe. Did I dare to get on one, even if I could? How else would I get up to the apartment?

A bell chimed. People behind pushed me against the people in front. I craned my neck to try to see inside the elevator as the dented metal doors slid open. Did I want to get on or not? All I could do was try to stay on my feet as I was dragged helplessly forward—falling would surely have meant being trampled to death.

And somehow I found myself right on the threshold, pushing to get out of the way of the elevator doors already sliding toward me. I thrust myself inside, stepping on toes, as the doors slammed. An alarm was ringing, probably indicating that the elevator was too full, but no one was going to get out. "Shut the damn thing off!" a deep voice rumbled like a tape played too slow.

"Please, let me out!" I begged them, uselessly.

The alarm ground to a stop. The elevator shuddered and began to ascend. I told myself that the elevator didn't have very far to fall, at this point. I would get off if it made it to the next floor, and wait for a less crowded one. Luckily, I was still close to the doors.

The elevator stopped. But the doors behind me didn't open—the doors on this floor were on the other side. How would I ever get off? "Wait! This is my—" I started to call out.

In a twinkling the elevator was empty. Then the doors slammed shut. I was alone. I pushed 3, Eve and Sylvan's floor, thankful for my sudden good luck. Maybe I still had a chance to get to their apartment in time.

But the elevator descended, ignoring my hand on the button, heading back to the basement, where I knew another crowd was waiting. I howled in frustration. But at least I knew where the doors would open on the first floor. I stayed beside them as the other doors opened behind me.

The basement was empty. So why had the elevator

gone back down here? Mystified, I pushed 3 again, re-
peatedly. It seemed to take the elevator twice as long as it
did the last time to get from the basement to the first floor,
even though it had been weighted down with all those
people then. Again, it stopped on 1, where no one had
been waiting a moment ago. But now people boiled on,
crushing me back against the other doors.

I watched the numbers over the door, people pressed
on all sides of me, cursing myself for not getting off this
thing when I had the chance. We quickly passed the
second floor. Would it stop on 3? I pushed the button like
crazy, but this elevator didn't seem to pay any attention to
that.

Miraculously, it did stop on 3. I rushed forward and
managed to get out, along with everybody else. The doors
slammed on an empty elevator. In a moment, the hallway
was empty, too.

This was crazy, one situation suddenly becoming another with no noticeable transition. But I couldn't worry
about that now. I'd try to figure it out later. First I had to
find the apartment.

The building had been drastically renovated, the hallway completely unfamiliar. I couldn't even tell which
way the front of the building was. Their apartment had
been 311 before. But how did I know the numbers hadn't
been changed, along with everything else?

All I could do was try to find 311. If it was the wrong
apartment, I would just have to knock on every door on
the third floor. The hallway stretched away on either side
of me, the same horrible ceiling lights flashing and stutter-

129

ing back and forth across the length of it. I went to the left, following my instincts. The fifth doorway was 311. I hesitated briefly, trying to prepare myself for whatever horribly unexpected thing would happen next. I pressed the bell.

There was no answer. I waited a decent length of time, then pressed it again, hearing the chime inside the apartment. It suddenly occurred to me that Eve and Sylvan could have been somewhere else, outside the apartment, when he phased us into the future. If so, the chances were pretty great that they would have ended up inside an object, and been killed. Even if they'd made the trip safely, they probably would be embroiled in some kind of mess. How would I ever find them? The effects of chaos made it almost impossible to get around inside this building. Things outside must have been a lot worse. I didn't even want to think about traffic.

And there was still the possibility that he hadn't sent them to this timeline at all.

I checked my watch, to see how long ago I'd left the apartment in my own timeline, how long I'd been in chaos. But the digital watch wasn't working right, it was moving in waves, the seconds blurring ahead so fast I couldn't see them, then freezing, blinking by as slowly as minutes. Chaos seemed to have peculiar effects on all kinds of machinery.

But maybe the watch wasn't malfunctioning—maybe time itself was. Eve had said something about time being peculiar in chaos. That could be why peoples' voices and movements kept speeding up and slowing down—time was flowing in irregular waves. It would have been interesting to think about, if I hadn't been in the middle of it. Now I tried to push the thought from my mind. I pressed the bell again. I lifted my hand to knock.

"Who's there?" asked a faint voice on the other side of the door.

The person inside must have been unable to see me through the tiny peephole because of the unsteady light. I couldn't hear the voice well enough to be able to tell if it was Eve or not. If it *wasn't* Eve, how was I going to convince her to open the door, so I could find out if they had ever been here? "My name is Max," I called out. "Please, it's kind of an emergency. I need to find some people who . . . who I think might have been here. I've got to help them. Their names are—"

The door clicked open a crack. An eye peered at me. The door swung wide. Eve stood there—unmistakably the real Eve, in the same baggy jeans and T-shirt she had been wearing when I last saw her, just a few hours ago, in this building. I moved toward her as relief flooded through me.

"*You!*" She hurled the word at me, and started to slam the door in my face.

But not before I had wedged my foot in it. Stronger than she was, I managed to push the door open again. I stepped inside and closed it behind me. "Thank God I found you," I said.

"Get out of here!" she screamed. "You did this to us. You're the only one who could have. I never want to see you, look at you again! You're a liar, a monster, a . . ." She couldn't find a word bad enough for me.

I started to tell her I was sorry, but realized before I did that any apology would be so puny in comparison to what I had done to them that it was better not to make one at all. I couldn't face her, and turned away.

The floor plan seemed to be the same as the apartment these two had lived in, but there were no cozy nooks. It was sparsely furnished, with an elaborate bar in one corner and a lot of empty floor space. The room seemed to have been set up for entertaining, rather than quiet evenings at home. And then I saw something so unexpected it was like a slap on the face.

"Huh?" I said, stepping toward a brightly colored photograph on the wall. The other Eve and Sylvan, deeply tanned, reclined by a pool somewhere, lifting glasses. They were, of course, smoking. "But . . ." I turned back to her. "This is *them*. It's the others. Does that mean this was their apartment too?"

"Don't pretend to be surprised. This is their apartment, in their timeline—or what's *left* of their timeline, after what they did to it. And now they're safe in *our* timeline, and we're trapped in the mess they made of their future, because of you." She made a sound of disgust. "It's just as if *we* got lung cancer and heart disease, because *they* smoked and drank."

"But are they really safe?" Even now, I wondered what was happening to the other Eve, always at the mercy of her maniac father, as I looked at her in the photograph. I turned away reluctantly. "Your father said they would drag our timeline into chaos too, because of not belonging there, being strange attractors."

"So I thought," Sylvan said from the kitchen doorway,

where he seemed to have been standing quietly since I had come inside. "But I may have been wrong. I was wrong about so many things. I didn't think the timelines would multiply so quickly. I didn't think Sylvan could safely send us to the future, but apparently he can. I thought their existence in our timeline would make it unstable, but maybe it won't—now that we're out of it. Maybe switching places with us was enough to make things safe for them there. At least . . . at least that would mean there's one stable timeline left, somewhere."

"And at least he *didn't* send us to the molten earth," I said, daring to look back at Eve.

"They might as well have! Get rid of him, Dad. I can't stand the sight of him."

"I understand how you feel, my dear," Sylvan said, moving slowly toward me now. I saw that he was holding a knife, a lot bigger and sharper-looking than the knife the woman had in the basement. It was a health-food cleaver! He must have been chopping something hefty like rutabagas when Sylvan phased him here. "I wonder if there is a penalty for murder, in chaos? An academic question, I suppose." He smiled to himself, approaching me.

15

I knew they would hate me. I also should have known that there would be no chance of our helping each other, after what I had done. But I hadn't expected Sylvan to go crazy. I backed away from him.

"Did he let you keep the phaser?" Sylvan asked me, lifting the cleaver. "Obviously you had one on you when you were here this afternoon."

"And we actually felt *sorry* for you, we felt *guilty* for getting you into this," Eve said, her voice thick with repugnance. She could barely get the words out, speaking in a peculiar kind of drone. "And you had our phaser the whole time, you were planning to . . ." She swallowed, unable to finish.

"No, of course he didn't let me keep it—even though he promised he would."

"Your reward, eh?" Sylvan said, still smiling, closer now, not lowering the cleaver. His voice began to speed up, rising in pitch. "So tell me, exactly how did you get us registered? What *was* your little strategy? I'm rather curious to know."

Sweat broke out on my forehead. Sylvan's smile was feral, demented. Would anything stop him from killing me? Maybe if I was completely honest he would give me a chance—or at least hesitate long enough to let me explain. "Wait a minute, listen," I begged him. "When I went to the bathroom, I jumped ahead sixteen hours, to when you were asleep. I did it then."

"And then, when you went back to him, he took the phaser away from you. He cheated you out of your reward." Sylvan's smile was beginning to fade. "That wasn't very nice of him, was it? After you had carried out your service to him so efficiently."

I backed up against the door, reaching for the knob. But I didn't want to run away from them; in chaos, I would never find them again. "I was registered on his phaser!" I blurted out. "He threatened to send me to the molten earth if I didn't do it. And he *would* have—that's what he's like. And he said . . . he said that helping him was the only way I could keep the phaser." I was panting now, as though I'd just run up several flights of stairs. "Do you

135

know what that feels like, the way the phaser attaches itself to you, like a part of your body? You would do anything, even . . . even the thing I did, to keep it." I stopped feeling for the doorknob; I knew I couldn't leave them. I had to stay and explain myself, even if Sylvan *was* about to kill me. Nothing mattered now but the truth. "Eve and I attacked him, we tried to get it away from him at the end, but he was just too fast." I lifted my head and faced Sylvan directly. "Go ahead, do what you want," I told him. "I'm not leaving this apartment."

"It really *does* seem to bother you. Perhaps you do have some human feelings after all," Sylvan said, wonderingly. "And you say you tried to get the phaser away from him in the end, tried to stop him? That was something, at least." He sighed. "A little late, that's all."

"I know, I *know!*" I shouted, banging my fists against the door. "But he was so incredibly *skillful* with the phaser, he had used it so much, he knew all the tricks. It was . . . irresistible, seeing what he could do with it. He hooked me, taught me a little; I *had* to learn more. And I won't even try to explain what else was wrong with me, this kind of *power* they had, the way they made me forget things, made me crazy. I wouldn't expect you to listen."

"Yes, they *are* strange attractors, aren't they," Sylvan said, watching me, his expression changing. "We never met them. But now I can see. The way they infiltrated Security so quickly. The kind of . . . effect they had on people."

"Oh, Dad, you're so soft you make me *sick!*" Eve screamed at him, pressing both hands to her ears. "I can't listen. If you start trying to understand him, I'll throw up! I'm going to lie down—assuming there's a bed to lie on." She marched off down the hall.

I moved away from the door and sank into a chair. Sylvan set the cleaver down on a table, his arm moving in slow motion. We looked away from each other in silence. Was it possible that he might someday begin to forgive me? I shouldn't hope for that. But I was struck by how very different he was from the other Sylvan. There was no artifice to him; his emotions were all right there to be seen. In that way, I almost felt a sort of kinship with him.

And what about Eve? What kind of influence had the fathers had on their daughters? Was the other one scheming and artificial and the real one honest? I refused to believe it was that simple. I still wanted to trust the other Eve. And I doubted that there was any chance this Eve would ever stop hating me. Why did I care so much?

"None of us will last very long, in any case," Sylvan said.

"What do you mean?"

He ran his hand through his hair, looking exhausted. "It's not just civilization falling apart. I don't see how organic life can last much longer in this timeline, the way it's going." He looked cautiously at his watch, then quickly covered it with his other hand, grimacing. "You must have noticed. Even *time* is turbulent here, moving in waves, in eddies. The discontinuities that keep—"

"Dad! *Dad!*" Eve shrieked from the hallway.

I jumped to my feet. There were a few other people in the apartment now, I noticed, shadowy figures in corners.

I hadn't seen them come in; they seemed to have been here for a while, like the people in the basement corridor.

Eve rushed into the room, grinning crazily at her father. She was clutching the teddy bear.

"Oh, my God," Sylvan whispered, his eyes on the bear. Then he added quickly, "Are you sure? Does she have others?"

"Not a one," Eve told him, breathing hard. "Everything else in the room is completely different."

"Then it *has* to be . . ."

"What happened? What's the matter with the bear?" I asked them. And I felt a sudden, inexplicable impulse to take the bear away from her.

The unfamiliar woman standing beside me reached toward Eve. "Aw, isn't he the *cutest* thing!" she said. "Can I hold him?"

Eve pulled the bear tightly against herself. "Who's she? Why did you let her in?" she accused me.

"I didn't. She was already inside the apartment. That's the way things happen here."

Eve and Sylvan looked nervously around. There was laughter now, and clinking glasses. "Mommy, I *want* that bear!" said the little boy who was with the unfamiliar woman.

"I'm sure the nice lady will let you play with it, dear," the woman assured him.

"Dad, what are we going to do?" Eve appealed to her father.

"Use it . . . somehow," Sylvan said unsurely.

"Eve, what *is* it about that bear?" I demanded, my hands tingling as I stared at it.

"Why should I tell *you?*"

"I think we *have* to, Eve. I don't know how to . . ." Sylvan pulled his eyes away from the bear. "Max. You registered the bear when you registered Eve, right?"

"As a matter of fact, I did," I said, confused. "It has the same specimen number. Why is that so important?"

"Mommy, I want that *bear!*" wailed the little boy.

"He'll make a scene if you don't let him hold it—and so will I," the woman threatened.

We tried to edge away from them, but it wasn't easy, the room was so crowded now. "Why did you do it, Max?" Sylvan wanted to know.

I shrugged, a little embarrassed. "Well, I just felt so bad about . . . about what I was doing, and I saw . . ." I looked away from them. "The way you were hugging that bear, while you were sleeping. I just thought I would register it, too. So it would travel with you. You know, to maybe give you a little comfort, wherever he was going to send you."

"Comfort?" Sylvan said, with a funny laugh. "It'll give us a lot more than that—if we ever get a chance to use it." He rubbed his hands together, his shoulders hunching as he looked around the room. His voice became urgent. "We've got to hurry. Do you think we can just go from here?"

"Is there something hidden *inside* the bear?" I asked, excitement rising within me, finally beginning to get it. "Something that begins with a P?"

"Oh, what fun, a guessing game!" cried the woman, clapping her hands. "If Bernie guesses, can he hold the bear?"

"Don't tell him, Dad!" Eve warned him. "He'd just—"

He ignored her. "I had two phasers," he told me. "One at the labs, one at home. This is where we hid it."

"You really *mean* it?" I shouted above the crowd, grabbing Sylvan's arm. It was almost too wonderful to believe—a phaser, and so close to me! "You're sure it's in there?"

He reached out for the bear, but Eve only clutched it more tightly, backing away. "Yes. I can feel it," she said, glaring at him, and turned to me. "Congratulations, Max. You finally did something right. But don't think we're going to take *you* back with us."

16

"Come on, Dad, don't just stand there! We can lock ourselves in the bathroom and go back from there."

"No, you *can't!*" I howled.

"Try and stop us! Hurry up, Dad!"

But Sylvan stayed rooted in place, wringing his hands, terrified of making such a drastic move.

I couldn't let them go back without me—for a lot of reasons. "Listen to me," I begged her. "I know how it works, I learned from the other one. You two have never used the phaser on yourselves before, have you?"

Sylvan shook his head. He had been too timid for that, and he was afraid of doing it now. His ignorance of the strategies of time travel was why they needed me, and he knew it. I just had to convince Eve.

"You *can't* just go back to your own time from here," I told them. "Time is all mixed up now. You'd never hit exactly the right instant, from chaos. Even if you got close, it's too risky. You'd end up in the middle of something, change the past, make a bifurcation. You'd just bring chaos back *with* you!"

"It's very rude to make a promise to a child and then back down," the woman admonished us. "Come on, Bernie. Think of something that starts with P."

"Ummm . . . Poo-poo!" Bernie cried, and shrieked with delight.

Sylvan, at least, recognized the logic of what I was saying. "But then how *can* we get back, without bringing chaos? Is there any way at all?" he asked me despairingly.

There was. More than ever now, I appreciated the other Sylvan's brilliance. 33,019 B.C. on the Great Plains was a buffer zone. It was an escape from chaos, and the only safe way to travel in time at all. You could head for it without fear of making a bifurcation. Even if you didn't hit exactly the right moment, there were no people around, no objects, nothing much happening to interfere with and change the past. And then, from stability and calm, you could very carefully jump into the future. Traveling to the future was less likely to make bifurcations.

"Don't be silly, Bernie," the woman said. "Now let me see . . . A penny? A pickle?"

"Yes, we can get back. I saw how he did it," I told Sylvan. "With hoverpacks we could go from right here, from anywhere. Without them, we have to go from ground level, from one particular place—and I know where it is. But it would be a lot easier with hoverpacks."

Eve was trying to pull Sylvan away. "Dad, don't listen to him! How can you ever trust him again?"

I looked frantically around. No one in the apartment seemed to be wearing a hoverpack. Did they have them here? I could check by looking outside; maybe we could find a place to buy them, here or in the future. "Wait right there," I told Sylvan. "I'll be back in a second. And believe me, if you use that thing without knowing what you're doing, you'll wreck the other timeline, too."

Fighting the craving to stay close to the phaser, I pushed roughly through the crowd to a window and looked out. There were people with hoverpacks all right, but I immediately gave up any idea of going outside to try to get some. Clouds seemed to appear and disappear; the sun blinked on and off like a strobe light over rows of automobiles, some abandoned, some with blaring horns, trapped in permanent gridlock. Many of the nearby buildings were nothing but rubble. Fires danced across the wreckage of what looked like futuristic airborne vehicles. Many people had guns, on the ground and in the air. A sudden burst of hail battered against the windowpane. I heard a scream above me, the whir of rotors. An arm fell past, the hand holding a half-eaten ice cream cone.

It was too dangerous out there to try to get hoverpacks. We had to go from the laundry room—if we could still get

143

to it. I worked my way back to Eve and Sylvan. They were gone. Cursing, I headed for the bathroom. Fortunately, someone was already locked inside. Eve was banging on the door, Sylvan cringing miserably beside her.

"Come with me. You're wasting time. We've got to get out of here," I shouted at them.

"I couldn't agree with you more," said a man brushing past me. "This party is a *bore*."

"Just leave us alone!" Eve screamed.

"Listen to me," I begged Sylvan. "We've got to go back to 33,019 B.C., near where Sylvan's hideout is. It's the only way to get home. And we have to go from basement level, or we'll die in the fall. I know exactly where we can travel safely from. Come on!"

"You said their hideout was in 43,000 B.C.," Eve reminded me.

"I was lying then, to protect them. It's 33,019, believe me."

"But why do we have to go back so far?" she demanded.

"It's empty. We won't make a bifurcation."

Sylvan closed his eyes, thinking, then nodded. "He's making sense, Eve," he said. "And going back there might also be the best way to . . . try to get rid of the other Eve and Sylvan."

"That's right," I said. But suddenly I wondered what we were going to have to do to the other Eve in order to get safely home.

"Get rid of them?" Eve blinked. That idea appealed to her more than any of my arguments. But still she resisted.

"You sure Max isn't trying to trick us? To go back with them and leave us here?"

Her stubbornness was maddening. How could I convince her? "Look, you can press the buttons," I said, though I didn't like the idea. "But if we don't go now, we might never even make it down to the basement."

"All right. Let's get out of here," she said. "But that *still* doesn't mean we're taking you back with us."

"Help us, please," the woman with the little boy begged us as we passed them. I saw now that she was dressed in rags, and that the child in her arms was emaciated, with a swollen belly. "Please, how can you deny a starving child?" she pleaded feebly. "It's just a toy to you, but it would mean so much to him . . ."

We hurried away from them. People were streaming in through the apartment door now, but once we pushed past them, the hallway was blissfully empty. I headed for the elevators, wishing there was another way to get down to the basement. Dust swirled along the floor; the air was full of smoke.

Just before we reached the elevators we passed a doorway with a hole chopped in it, as though with an ax. I peered through—at a flight of stairs. "Come on, this way," I said. "Somebody did us a big favor. We don't want to take the elevators if we can help it."

But the stairs were not much better than the elevators. On some flights, we had to push against the crowd moving up; on others, everyone else was going down, and people kept trying to get in between us. Eve and Sylvan, clinging together, were below me now, the phaser farther away from me. "Wait! You'll never get there without me!" I yelled down at them. Sylvan looked back, not wanting to lose me in the unpredictable crowd; Eve pushed determinedly ahead.

The stairway trembled, then swayed. There were screams, and several people fell. Would we even make it to the basement before the building collapsed? I started to help a little girl to her feet, but a woman pulled her violently away from me. I pushed ahead, doggedly, trying to keep my eyes on Eve and Sylvan, who were passing the landing and turning onto the next flight.

The door to the basement had been battered down. I worked my way through, into the elevator lobby. Then I panicked, unable to see Eve and Sylvan in the crowd. Bells chimed. All three elevators opened at once. People rushed from one to another. The group around me surged toward the middle one. I kicked people, punched them, pushed them in the face, fighting my way toward the corridor that led to the laundry room, yelling for Eve and Sylvan.

And Sylvan called my name, waving his hand in the air. "Into that corridor!" I screamed. "And then *wait* for me!"

The basement was a little less crowded away from the elevators, and at last I reached Eve and Sylvan. "This way," I told them.

"But how do we know you're not—"

"Just shut up and come with me!"

Sylvan grabbed Eve's arm and pulled her along. We hurried toward the laundry room, people thinning out around us. The mosslike carpeting had pulled apart in sticky strands above deep cracks in the floor. The ground heaved again; the three of us careened into the wall. We kept going. There was more smoke in the air here; it was becoming uncomfortably hot. And then I saw that the smoke was billowing from the laundry room doorway.

We stopped outside it, panting. "We can't go in there," I said stupidly.

"For *this* he dragged us all the way down here?" Eve said to her father. "We'd be much better off on our—"

"Shut up and let me think!" I held my breath and looked into the laundry room, trying to get an idea of the exact spot where I had landed, which was in the same space as the mobile home living room in 33,019 B.C. Of course, we didn't want to travel from that spot; we wanted to land outside the mobile home. "Follow me," I ordered them, and ran a dozen yards back toward the elevators. "This ought to be safe enough," I said, when they reached me. "Hurry. Get out the phaser." I was desperate to see it again.

They looked at each other. There was a sound like thunder in the distance, though I knew it wasn't thunder. Sylvan reached for the bear, his hands trembling. But Eve wouldn't give in. "No. You'll just give it to Max," she said, pushing his hands away. She turned her back to me, fumbling with the bear. She pulled a phaser out of it—it was all I could do not to grab it away from her—and then she dropped the bear carelessly on the floor.

"Hey, don't do that," I said, immediately picking up the bear. "You've got to keep this."

"Why? Who needs it now?" she said, still turned away from me.

147

"If we ever get back, you've got to sleep with it that night. If you don't have it then, I won't be able to register it. Then we wouldn't have the phaser now. We wouldn't be able to get away. We should register it with you now, on this phaser, just to make sure."

"He's right, Eve," Sylvan said. "Now let me have the phaser."

"Tell me what buttons to push!"

"You don't know how to use it. You're just wasting time. Give it to me," he told her, in a tone of voice I'd never heard him use with her before.

No one ever wanted to give up a phaser. Eve sighed, but she turned back and resolutely handed it over. He switched it on, then looked at me. "Now . . . we register ourselves?" he said, with great reluctance.

"Yes. Hurry."

But he did nothing. I touched the strip myself, barely resisting the impulse to pull it away from him. I handed the bear to Eve. "Now you touch it, and touch the bear to it at the same time. Then at least it will always stay in the same time as you. But the phaser won't keep it with you in space, remember that. That's why you must never put it down, until we're safe."

She hesitated for a moment, then pressed her lips together and touched her finger and the bear's paw to the phaser. She jerked back a little at the sensation.

Sylvan swallowed, but brought himself to touch it at last. "Now, where . . . where do you suggest we go, exactly?" he asked me, wiping his forehead with a grimy hand, looking miserable at the thought of actually using the phaser.

But he did seem to trust me, at least. I tried to think logically, which wasn't easy. The flames spouting from the laundry room doorway would freeze weirdly for an instant, then spring to life again as the time waves passed them. The heat was becoming unbearable. "Well, when I was with them there, it was 33,019 B.C. But maybe we should go back before then, before they ever got there, so we won't run into them—if Sylvan sees us, this time he *will* send us to the molten earth. And traveling from here, where time is so turbulent, we could easily miscalculate; we've got to have a big margin of error. So maybe we should go all the way back to . . . maybe as far as 43,000 B.C., and plan the next move from there."

"You're just trying to trap us," Eve said. "That's where you said their hideout was in the first place. That's probably where it *really* is."

"No, it's *not!*" I insisted, wishing I had never lied to them. "I can't run into Sylvan either. I know too much. He wants to kill me, too. He sent me here, didn't he? If we're going to avoid him, we *have* to go back to 43,000 B.C."

"You think so?" Sylvan said doubtfully, his hair standing out in tufts around his damp face.

"You got a better idea?"

"I . . . I guess not." Sylvan pressed keys, slowly and carefully. I longed to grab it from him and do it myself. The building swayed; dust and broken plaster from the ceiling sprinkled down on us.

"You're really going to take him? After what he did?" Eve said.

He rose toward her. "We got him into this. Do you

really want me to leave him here?" he asked her, his tone angry again.

She looked down at the floor. "No. I . . . I guess not."

"Gee, thanks," I said.

"*Not* because I'll ever forgive you. Only because we need your help." She was reluctant to admit even that much.

"Well, let's go then, before this whole place caves down on us," I urged Sylvan. "Come on, press ACTIVATE."

His hand, poised over the key, was trembling more than ever. Even now, he was terrified of using it. I reached over and pressed ACTIVATE myself.

17

Darkness. Silence. Icy wind lifting my hair. The stars overhead.

Eve and Sylvan, disoriented, sprawled on their hands and knees. I sank down onto the grass beside them. Despite the cold, the space and emptiness were an inexpressible relief. For a long moment, no one spoke.

I looked around, my eyes adjusting to the night. I could see no sign of the mobile home. I turned back, checking quickly to make sure the phaser was still in Sylvan's hand. "Where are we, exactly?" I asked him.

"Huh? Oh. Oh, yes." He sat up on his knees, and put his shaking hand to his forehead, then studied the phaser: "42,399 B.C."

We had missed the target date by 601 years. Was it because we had traveled from chaos, or had Sylvan also miscalculated? If only they would trust me to carry the phaser! "We're going to have to hit it closer next time, or we'll ruin everything," I said.

Eve looked around, shivering. "Can we go home now?" she asked.

I wanted to go home too. And I wanted to see the other Eve again—though that was probably impossible. I was going to have to face the fact of what we had to do to the other Eve and Sylvan now; in chaos, there had been no time to worry very much about that. "I don't think we can just . . . blunder back into our present, with the others there. We've got to surprise Sylvan somehow, trap him, get him registered before he knows it, before he sees us. Otherwise, he'll just get rid of us. Instantly."

"But *how?*" Sylvan said, his voice ragged. "How can we *ever* register him, without his knowing it? It's not possible. He'll get us first. We're no better off than we were before."

"We're not in chaos. And we have a phaser. There must be *something* we could do," I said, trying to sound more positive than I felt. I kept looking back at the phaser, glowing dully in Sylvan's palm, itching to get my hands on it.

"Why can't we just go home, one second after he sent us away, and lock ourselves in and then report him to the police?'' Eve suggested. ''And then, after they've got him in custody, and taken the phaser away from him, we can register him and . . . and . . .'' Her voice faded. ''No,'' she said. ''That wouldn't work. He would escape with it first, as soon as we tried anything.''

''You're right,'' I told her. She was catching on fast. ''He can always escape. As soon as he has the slightest hint that we're back—he wouldn't even have to *see* us, to know—he'll send us 4.5 billion years into the past. There's nothing to stop him.'' I got to my feet and began pacing.

''Wouldn't we have a better chance in 33,019 B.C., surprising him at his hideout?'' Eve said slowly. ''He won't be as careful or as cautious there, with no one else around.''

''That's a great idea!'' And it was. I was impressed and thankful for her quick grasp of strategy. ''His hideout is where he's most vulnerable.''

''Yes, but even back at his hideout, as soon as he catches a glimpse of us, that'll be the end,'' Sylvan argued.

''Well . . .'' I was thinking hard now. ''We could work our way carefully to 33,019, always staying in the middle of the night, so he won't see us. We can just keep watching, and find a time when he isn't there. You can tell by whether the car's there or not, the Jeep Cherokee. Now, he sent us into chaos . . .'' I paused, trying to remember. ''It was around 1 P.M., June 26. When he traveled between his hideout and the twentieth century, he usually kept the time and date the same, he told me—you can burn out fast if you don't do that. So, we could head for

153

June 26, 33,019 B.C., soon after dark. He might be away then, settling into your apartment. We could get inside the mobile home—I don't think he even bothered to lock it—wait for him there, and register him the instant he walks through the door. He'd never expect that.''

''It might work,'' Eve said. ''But we'd have to move really fast. Two of us would have to grab him, immobilize him just long enough for the other one to press the buttons. You said he was quick.''

''That's true,'' I said. She was smarter, and her survival instincts were even sharper than I had realized. ''But remember, he'd be off his guard. We might have a chance, if we knew ahead of time exactly who was going to do what.''

There was a long silence. ''I don't know if my nerves could take the tension,'' Sylvan finally said, sounding old. ''And I don't like using the phaser any more than absolutely necessary.''

''Would you rather be in chaos?'' I asked him. ''We're going to have to do *something* risky like that, or give up.''

He sighed heavily. ''I suppose you're right. But if we ever get back—we must *never* use the phaser again.''

''Sure, sure,'' I said. There was no point in arguing with him about that now.

''Well, let's just do it then, and get it over with,'' said Eve, getting to her feet.

She certainly had guts. ''Fine with me,'' I said. Now I had to convince them to let me be the one to carry the phaser. ''But first we have to—''

''Can't we just rest for a little while?'' Sylvan asked, still on the ground. "There's no immediate emergency. I've got to . . . to take some time to catch my breath."

"Fine," I said. I did want a chance to be alone briefly, and think, though it was an effort to put any distance between myself and the phaser. I strolled away from them, not very far, looking at the sky, my hands in my pockets. And I saw, in the distance, a great dark cliff looming across the entire horizon. The retreating glacier, which would come back, thousands of years from now, to crush what was left of the hideout.

Behind me, Eve and Sylvan began to whisper. Were they plotting against me? They could kill me at any moment, with the touch of a key. But I doubted that they would. It was not only that they needed me. I also knew that they were basically decent. I trusted them.

In that respect, they were the exact opposite of the others. I remembered the evening at the prehistoric hideout—the exotic food, the vibrant attraction of Eve, the thrill and adventure of flying to 1910 Bangkok. I couldn't help but compare it to the real Eve and Sylvan's cozy, cluttered, but ordinary apartment, their health-food diet, their reluctance to explore the exciting possibilities of the phaser. I knew that siding with them was the right thing to do, that I had no choice. But I also felt a pang at what I was giving up. It was the difference between a life of eating steak and a life of eating bean curd.

If I had never met the other Eve, and had had that taste of adventure, I wouldn't have compared things in this way. It was all the result of my running out of the house yesterday morning without answering the second phone call, when the real Eve had tried to reach me. Such a small thing, but such a tremendous difference in the end: Sensitive dependence on initial conditions, the first rule of chaos. If I had answered that phone call, I would have gone to the apartment instead of the waterfall house; I probably never would have met the other Eve at all.

And I never would have made the unforgivable mistake of registering the real Eve and Sylvan.

And yet, there was still a crazy part of me that wanted to see the other Eve again. I knew there would never be time, but I wished I could have just a few minutes alone with her, a chance to explain my feelings—before sending her away forever. To tell her that I had to do it, to save our timeline, and because her father was *wrong*. And that—

Sunlight burst across the sky. I shrank away from it, shielding my eyes, stumbled and almost fell. I felt as though I had just staggered off an amusement-park ride. My heart racing, I carefully took my hand away from my eyes and looked around. It was a little warmer, but still impossible to tell what year, century, or millennium I had landed in.

I could hardly believe the real Eve and Sylvan had done this. Despite how competent Eve was, I knew—and *they* knew—that they needed me in order to get safely home. It didn't make any sense, and yet obviously they had sent me to another time. But why?

"Max!" someone called.

I spun around. There was the mobile home, fifty feet away, the Jeep Cherokee parked beside it.

"Max!"

The voice was coming from above. I looked up. Eve fell toward me in a hoverpack, a phaser in her hand. She wore her black jumpsuit. The reflecting objects on her cheeks were tears, sparkling like jewels in the sunlight. "Oh, Max, I found you! I found you in time!"

When she hugged me, it was just as it had been before; stunned as I was, my arms slipped around her with quick inevitability. But we didn't stand there for very long. She pulled me into the mobile home, sat beside me on the white canvas couch—and told me what she had done to her father.

"It was horrible, Max. The look on his face when I did it! But I *had* to. Everything changed when I saw what he did to you, when I saw how he'd been lying to me all along."

"This is really the truth, Eve?" I asked her, hardly believing it. "You sent your father back 4.5 billion years?"

She nodded silently at me, biting her lip.

"Really?"

"Max?" She seemed a little wounded now. "You act like you don't believe me, don't trust me."

I laughed uncomfortably. As dangerous and uncontrollable as Sylvan had been, I was still shocked that she had done this to her own father. "You have to understand, it's kind of a lot to take in all at once," I said, "I mean, your father suddenly out of the picture, for good. Me being here with you. I *want* to trust you. But you did . . . play some tricks on me before."

"I know," she admitted, looking down. "That phony phaser Dad planted in 1910 Bangkok, that whole scheme to get you on our side."

"Phony phaser? What do you mean?" I *had* wondered what a phaser was doing in 1910 Bangkok.

"Oh, Dad set it all up in advance," she said. "He paid those two men to meet there and exchange the package, knowing the lightning would kill them, knowing it would lead to a chaotic timeline somewhere." She pushed back her hair, which didn't want to stay braided but stood out in messy wisps around her face. "He figured you wouldn't help us unless you believed he was gong out of his way to save the timelines from the phaser. Plus, he thought you'd enjoy the trip—and you did, I *know* you did."

"But . . . but you lied to me, you went along with it."

She got up and lit a cigarette, gripping the phaser in one hand, pacing. "But it was survival, Max. And I *never* thought he would send you into chaos with the others. He promised, and I believed him. I guess I should have known better." She sat down on the couch beside me again. "But I *found* you before it was too late." She brightened, regaining some of her old sparkle. "It's almost too wonderful to believe."

Did I dare trust her? Why *would* she bring me back here if Sylvan were still around and this were just some kind of scheme? There would have been no practical function to it. The only reason that made sense was what she was telling me—that she wanted to be with me. But I was still full of doubts and questions. I looked at the phaser in her hand, wanting it. "Is that the one he got from me or the one he already had?"

"It's the one he got from you." She stared down at it, biting her lip. "He had already registered himself on it. All I had to do was . . . press the keys."

That meant that I was registered on this phaser. The other Eve and Sylvan were also on it. Something else important was registered on it too. At the moment, I couldn't remember what it was. "But didn't it bother you, doing that to your father?"

"I was afraid of him, Max, of the crazy part of him. You know that."

"But how did you surprise him? He was always so quick."

She looked past me. "I watched him for two hours after he sent you away, until he turned his back on a phaser and I got my hands on it. And as soon as he was gone, I started looking for your specimen number, and *found* you!

I was so afraid something might have happened to you in chaos." She squashed the cigarette, put the phaser down carefully beside her on the couch, and reached out to me, as if for comfort. "Max, I don't want to think about Dad now."

Eventually we had something to eat—the leftovers from the meal she made on the night we flew to 1910 Bangkok. She gave me a jacket of Sylvan's, and we went outside to watch the sunset. I had gotten what I had wished for—a chance to be with her. But my emotions were a mess.

I still hadn't told her that the others had a phaser.

I didn't know what to do about that, so I kept putting it off. My arm tightened around her as the last red pinpoint shrank below the horizon. The sky was filling up with towering clouds, amazingly beautiful in the dying light. "So what happens next?" I asked her.

She put her head on my shoulder. "Do we have to think about that now? We have all the time in the world to make plans. I just want to relax for a while."

It would have been nice to relax with her, but I couldn't, knowing what she had done—and knowing the others could show up at any moment. It was still June 26. Would they actually find their way here tonight, as I had suggested to them 10,000 years ago? I knew that I was essentially lying to Eve by not telling her the others had a phaser, and that they were close to us in space, in 42,399 B.C. But if I told her, she would have sent them back 4.5 billion years.

What was I going to do? I had wanted so much to be

with Eve again. I had regretted the life of adventure I was giving up. Now here we were, standing together in the wind under this dramatic sky, with all the time in the world. And what was I thinking about? The real Eve and Sylvan. They wouldn't stop haunting me.

"I'm restless, Max. Let's go for a drive before it starts to rain," Eve said. "I just have to lock the place up." She fumbled with keys and phaser, making sure the mobile home door was locked, and I wondered what that might mean in relation to the others. When she stepped back to me she made a frustrated gesture with the phaser. "I never know where to put this thing, and it always gets in the way," she complained. "None of my pockets are big enough—Dad always carried it. But I can't just leave it lying around."

In the car, she set it carefully on the dashboard and started the motor. She drove slowly. The childish little unraveling braid seemed so wrong on her, a jarring contrast to her heavily made-up eyes, her clinging, sophisticated jumpsuit. But it did not detract in any way from her appeal. I couldn't keep my eyes off her.

She stopped the car at the crude wooden ramp that led to the parking place in the twentieth century. "It's wonderful being back here, safe, with you," she said thoughtfully, staring out at the ramp. "But I doubt that we'll want to stay in total seclusion here for the rest of our lives." Her eyes slid toward me briefly, then back outside. "We'll spend a lot of time at the waterfall house. It'll be fun fixing it up. We can have parties there."

I agreed, hollowly. But what was really going to happen? What should I tell her about the others? What would she do if they suddenly did show up? She would *have* to get rid of them—two Eves together with phasers would really make a mess of the one normal timeline. It could easily happen, and I didn't want to think about it. "That ramp is pretty clever," I said, making conversation to distract myself. "It must have taken your father awhile to build it."

"He didn't build it himself. He got robots from the future to do it. We had a lot of fun, watching them. It was really amazingly brilliant of him, the way he . . ." Her voice faded. "Now I'm sorry we came here. I don't want to think about him. Anyway, it's starting to rain. The mud can be awful. Let's go back. We can get high. There's some great pot in the freezer."

The storm was upon us with surprising swiftness, lightning, thunder, rain pelting against the car roof. It reminded me of that night in Bangkok. What was I going to do? What was I going to tell her?

"You seem so quiet, Max," Eve said, leaning forward at the wheel, her eyes on the rain-streaked windshield and the blurred headlight beams. We were bumping along very slowly; she wasn't used to driving on this rough terrain, and had to keep shifting, concentrating on what she was doing.

"Quiet?" I said. "Am I? I guess . . . I'm just sort of stunned. It all happened so fast. I never expected to get out of chaos. I never thought I'd see you again."

She turned to smile at me. The car lurched. She looked ahead again, swearing under her breath, and shifted. The gears made a grinding protest. "I've got to be careful," she muttered. "No auto mechanics around here. We'd never be able to pull this thing up that ramp." She thought for a moment, then threw back her head and laughed, her face radiant. "Of course, we can always just buy a new car. We've got plenty of money. Oh, Max, we can do anything we want from now on!"

Her happiness was infectious. The possibility of a life of adventures with her blossomed in my mind like a jungle of exotic flowers. On the dashboard, the phaser glinted at me. If only I could stop torturing myself and just share it with her! I could still have everything it promised.

But it wasn't the way I had imagined it. I couldn't stop worrying about what she had done to her father; I couldn't stop worrying about the others. What am I going to do? I kept asking myself, over and over again. What am I going to do?

"Here we are," Eve said with relief, as the back of the mobile home appeared dimly out of the rain ahead. She turned the wheel, moving the car around toward the front. "I've got to be careful now, there's a big rut somewhere right around here," she said, slowing down. "Don't want to get stuck in the mud."

I saw them an instant before she did—Eve and Sylvan standing by the front door, frozen in terror in the headlight beams. They had been trying to get in. They hadn't seen us approaching from the other side of the mobile home, hadn't heard us in the thunder and the rain.

"How the hell did they get here?" Eve shrieked. She looked at me, horrified, gripping the wheel. "My God, they must have had an extra phaser." The car plunged into the rut. Eve swore again, shifting into reverse. The squealing tires spat out mud, the car rocked, but didn't move. "Do it, Max! Take the phaser and get rid of them!"

I grabbed the phaser. It fit so naturally in my hand. The relief, the comfort, the excitement of holding it again raced through me.

I looked back at Eve and Sylvan. They couldn't see into the car; they must have thought the other Sylvan was here. Eve was clutching the teddy bear. Slowly, Sylvan put his arm around her. They weren't even trying to run, to escape with their phaser. They knew Sylvan could get them from anywhere. They huddled together, squinting against the headlight beams, totally vulnerable. I was looking directly into the faces of people who knew they were about to die.

And then I remembered what else was registered on the phaser in my hand.

"What's the matter, Max? 4.5 billion years. *Do it!*"

She wouldn't hesitate at all to send them there, and didn't see why I should hesitate either. Thinking carefully, I touched the keys. I turned toward her. "Max?" she said, suddenly sounding scared.

"I have to do this, Eve," I said. "It's not because I want to, or because I don't care about you."

"What are you talking about? Just get rid of them!"

My finger didn't want to, but I gritted my teeth and willed it to press ACTIVATE. "Goodbye, Eve," I gasped, struggling for breath. I felt as though I was fighting a powerful undertow; it took all the strength I had to push

165

open the door. "I'll never forget you," I said, meaning it, and fell out backwards into the mud, the phaser in my hand, my eyes still on her.

"No!" she screamed, fear and rage and loss spilling across her face as she reached out to me. "Come back, Max! You can still—"

The car and the headlights blinked out of existence. All that remained of them was a fading streak across my eyes. There was nothing in the world but darkness and mud and rain.

Did I change the past when I sent her away in 33,019 B.C.? Did she change the past when she did it to her father? I thought about that a lot at first. I discussed it with Eve and Sylvan over and over, and I kept looking for alterations in the timeline. But it is so boring and ordinary in this timeline that it's not easy to tell if anything has changed at all. I now think Eve is right. It is not the world that is different, but only my perception of it.

My scientific career is assured, with Sylvan and his influence behind me. Eve and I spend a lot of time working together in his lab. She is truly brilliant, and will probably turn out to be a more distinguished scientist than I could ever hope to be. She trusts me as much as her father does now, and we have become very close. It's great to be friends with someone whom you can go to with almost any problem, and she will come up with practical, down-to-earth advice. When I told her I wanted to go look at the waterfall house one last time, she said it would only upset me. And right away—as if she'd known—she gave me a gift, a wonderful book of mathematical puzzles, which did help to distract me a little.

It no longer surprises me that they were able to find the right moment in 33,019 B.C. on their own. Eve has a special intuition about time travel. The most amazing and wonderful thing is that all three of us got back from chaos, working together, without making any noticeable or dangerous changes in the timeline. That's what gives me hope.

Eve says she didn't sleep at all the night we got back, lying in bed with the teddy bear, waiting for me to touch her with the phaser. Sylvan, exhausted, did fall asleep in his study. He was so dazed when I woke him that he tried to keep me from locking the bathroom door, even though I'd told him it had to be that way. He had a little problem explaining to the locksmith how the door could be locked from the inside when nobody was in the room.

Sylvan, of course, destroyed both phasers. There was no way to talk him out of it. He dismantled them slowly and carefully, piece by piece. I watched in barely controlled agony, as though I were observing someone dissecting my own limbs. I could feel it throughout my entire nervous system when each phaser ceased to function.

But somehow, despite my extreme physical discomfort, I was also able to concentrate on what he was doing. I didn't take notes because it would have made them suspicious, but that night I wrote everything down. I have a pretty solid understanding of the circuitry.

They think I sent the other Eve to the molten earth. But I didn't. I just sent her ahead a few weeks. Without a phaser, she can't do anything to hurt them. But if *I* had a phaser I could go back, and explain, and we could even spend some time together in 33,019 B.C.

I can't discuss it with this Eve, of course. I know what she would say. She would tell me the only reason I want to go back is that the other Eve is a strange attractor, pulling the timeline toward chaos. But that isn't it. I just need to talk to her, to explain, to see her one more time. It wouldn't be enough of a change to bring on chaos. I know I'm right about that. I *have* to be.

Because I'm building a phaser now.